Truly thy friend,
Wm. P. Pinkham.

THE

LAMB OF GOD

OR THE

SCRIPTURAL PHILOSOPHY

OF THE

ATONEMENT

BY

WILLIAM P. PINKHAM, A. M.

MINISTER OF THE GOSPEL

To those noble
young men and young women
who now, in such numbers,
are consecrating themselves to God for
faithful and enduring service,
and who, to this end, are
seeking the light of His truth, this
volume is lovingly dedicated
by the author.

PREFACE.

THE following pages are written with an earnest desire to set forth clearly and helpfully the ground of the Christian's hope. The effort is a sincere and humble response to the oft-repeated request of those who have heard this exposition of Bible truth presented by word of mouth. It is not an exhaustive treatise, and it may embrace little that will be new to the well-instructed Christian. No attempt has been made to consider *all* that is included in the Savior's work for us, His sacrificial death, in its primary significance as our propitiation, being the point chiefly in view. It is hoped, however, that many a seeker after truth will here find light upon some of his difficulties respecting the way of salvation; and even that mature disciples will experience new assurance and new joy as again they "survey the wondrous cross."

The reader is requested to peruse this book

prayerfully and studiously, observing the Scripture references with care.

A few related subjects which could not properly be introduced into the body of the work, are treated in brief appendices, which may prove helpful to the understanding or the faith of some, and which are commended to the reader's earnest attention.

W. P. P.

PREFACE TO SECOND ISSUE.

I acknowledge my deep gratitude to my heavenly Father for many evidences that my little book has had a blessed ministry; that because of it my Lord is better known and loved and served. To Him be glory.

The new issue is not different from the former one, except in the correction of errors, the addition of a few sentences, and a new Analytical Index, as an aid to the study.

W. P. P.

GENERAL OUTLINE.

Appendices.

CHAPTER I.

INTRODUCTION.

THE vast army of young Christians marshalled under the name, or in the character, of Societies of Christian Endeavor, is to me an inspiration. It calls forth my most earnest prayers. To its ranks I look for great exploits in the conflict of the church against sin. Thence are to come the ministers, teachers, missionaries, who, with advantages that have fallen to no other generation, are to storm the fortresses of indolence, ignorance and crime; and, with an effectiveness unknown since the apostles, proclaim the Gospel to every creature. These are to reform society, purify government, unify the nations, herald the advent, usher in peace.

But whether their history shall be that of continuous victory, or of frequent vicissitude and defeat; whether the ultimate triumph shall be hastened or be long delayed, will depend very largely upon the readiness of the individual soldier to clothe himself with the panoply of war—"*the whole armor of God.*"* It will not be sufficient that he have "the

---

*In this book italics in quotations from the Bible are for emphasis.

hope of salvation," "the breastplate of righteousness," and "the shield of faith," essential as these
certainly are to successful warfare.   He must also
have the girdle of truth, "the preparation of the
Gospel of peace," and "the sword of the Spirit, which
is the word of God."

Veteran soldiers of the cross know well the cunning craftiness with which the followers of Satan
substitute plausible notions for the clear teachings
of the Holy Scriptures, plausible interpretations of
Scripture even, for that self-consistent and logically
impregnable system of truth, which was once delivered to the saints; and which has in its favor the
concurrent testimony of the great body of believers
of every succeeding age.

A host of Godless isms clamor against the servant
of Christ. Some of them wear the garb of truth, and
seem so like Christianity itself, that one is tempted
to think them at least harmless. But once admitted
to the chambers of the heart, they begin their sad
work of replacing faith with doubt, zeal with indif-
ference, and the sweet peace of God with a vain
conceit of knowledge.   It is the old story of Flat-
terwell, who knocked at the door of a goodly castle
and humbly asked admission, swearing that he
was friendly and alone; but once admitted by the

irresolute porter, whose fears he had disarmed with kindly words, he was followed by a swarthy retinue, bent upon pillage and murder. Many a child of God has not only become useless on God's side, but has lent his energies to the direct service of sin, and even made shipwreck of faith, by admitting into his belief, in moments of unwatchfulness, some beautiful speculation of whose true nature he was not aware.

The conservation and proper use of all that holy energy which is imparted to the believer at conversion, requires a clear understanding of the "principles of the doctrine of Christ." Such an understanding is not to be reached through the avowed enemies of Christianity; nor yet through those of the Christian name whose conceptions of Christ and of his word preclude the experience of his life-giving power. Societies exist, some of them under the name of churches, which deny the Lord that bought them. These cannot be trusted to interpret for us the Scriptures that testify of Him. They are willing to meet true Christianity part way, by admitting that the Bible contains, in some sense, a revelation of God; but that sense is to be determined by the reason of men; and, deny it as they will, they make human wisdom the final arbiter in questions of religion.   They meet Christianity part way by using freely its phraseology ; but even to its most important and distinctive terms they attach a meaning which would rob the Gospel of all that vitality and that exquisite finish which make it " sharper than any two-edged sword."

Evangelical churches, on the contrary, regard the Bible as infallible in its teachings, and as the supreme outward rule of faith and practice.   They insist that it is a product of Divine inspiration. They make the Bible itself and the Holy Spirit, who witnesses with it, its only true interpreters ; and they refuse to abandon its plain, simple statements, and its all comprehending, self-consistent system, for the allurements of pretended philosophy or the thrusts of opposing criticism.   They cling to that interpretation of Scripture which makes it "mighty through God to the pulling down of strongholds ;" which has, in every age and among all peoples, brought conviction of sin, furnished the repentant a well-grounded hope, reformed and transformed society.

The center and foundation of the true Christian faith is Christ crucified for us.   The atonement made by Him is the one great transaction of history. In its light every other transaction is to be judged, and every doctrine. Every failure to grasp the truth of God respecting this great transaction, is a failure to be able to interpret correctly a part—perhaps the greater part—of the Holy Scriptures. On the other hand, almost every portion of our blessed Bible glows with a new wealth and splendor of meaning in the light of the unveiled cross. To miss this is to miss all that is best in Divine revelation. To have this is to be powerfully fortified against errors of belief or conduct.

Of the many who profess the Christian religion, notably those who most fully exhibit the triumphs of grace, the fruits of the Spirit, and the power to prevail w:th God and men, are those who have caught that conception of the significance of Christ's death, in which all other just conceptions of it are involved, or to which they are secondary. That one conception, impressed Divinely and indelibly by the experience of salvation, becomes the true and effectual touchstone of belief and practice. Through this, bigotry, superstition, foolish philosophies and formularies are, and are to be, discovered and rejected, until the Church of Christ shines forth " as the morning, clear as the sun, fair as the moon, and terrible as an army with banners."

To see and know Jesus, then, in the light in

which God through the Holy Scriptures would reveal Him, is the potent secret of preservation and
of victory to the Christian disciple or the Christian
church. In our search for this knowledge may we
find help in the prayerful study of the following
pages.

CHAPTER II.

UNIVERSALITY OF SIN.

"For all have sinned and come short of the glory of God."
—Rom. 3, 23.

WHY is it that in seeking to present the most inspiring subject which the human mind can contemplate, we begin with facts the most melancholy and repulsive? It is because the skill of the Physician can be appreciated by those only who understand the complexity and malignity of the disease which he endeavors to remedy. The skill of the craftsman may be evinced in the beauty and utility of his handiwork; but it appears more remarkable and more praiseworthy when we know the extreme difficulties that beset his undertaking, and that he alone had the courage, the devotion and the ability to meet those difficulties and overcome them. Redemption cannot be rightly studied, apart from the thought of human sin and sinfulness.

The student, therefore, who would see the King in His beauty, and be ready to join in heartfelt hosannas to the Son of David, must very studiously examine those facts over which the Son of David has triumphed. It is meet, then, to begin with the above text, and to consider faithfully and prayerfully the sad fact which that text presents to us.

Sin, sin everywhere. Sin in the heart, on the tongue, in the actions. Sin in the bar-room, the theater, the ballroom, the gambling-den. Sin behind the counter and in front of it. Sin in palace and hovel, city and country. Sin in the state and in the church. Sin in legislator, judge, jury, clerk and constable. Sin in confessional and cloister, clergyman and layman. Sin in the little child and the man of gray hairs.

A race marked with sin. "Not a just man upon earth that doeth good and sinneth not."* "No man that sinneth not."† "They are all together become filthy; there is none that doeth good, no, not one."‡ "Jews and Gentiles * * all under sin."** Thus saith the Lord, whose word standeth forever. "If we say we have not sinned, we make Him a liar, and His word is not in us."††

But the conscience of man bears witness also.‡‡ Persons are found who, in resisting the appeals of God's messengers, say, "I don't know that I am a sinner." But if these same persons hear a minister preach holiness as a state to be known in this life,

---

*Eccl. 7, 20.　†1 Ki. 8, 46.　‡Ps. 14, 3.　**Rom. 3, 9.　††1 Jno. 1, 10.　‡‡Rom. 2, 15.

they are ready to exclaim, " Show me a holy man ; I never saw one." So they acknowledge sin in all others, though professedly blind to its existence in themselves. So, indeed, do they condemn themselves, unless they assume a superiority to all others.

The universality of sin among men has been acknowledged by Heathens, by Jews and by Christians. Both philosophy and religion have sought a remedy and a preventive. Generally they have sought in vain. There is but one exception, and that is Christianity. Its triumph is as yet but limited, because its acceptance is but limited ; but it—and it only—contains the promise of victory and answers the test of experiment.

Yet while Christianity is seeking to bring light and joy, and righteousness, and salvation to the world, all the powers of darkness are arrayed against it. Not a soul to whom the Gospel comes, but does in some sense, in some degree, at some time, resist its offers and invitations—another proof that the human race, to a man, is marked with sin.

Why is sin thus universal? And why this resistance to the only well attested ground of hope, the only plan which, with all the majesty of Divine authority, offers us pardon and cleansing, complete reconciliation to God, and unbounded enjoyment of

God? By the light of God's own word we shall
see.

But, whatever we shall find to be the cause
of the universality of sin, it is well to mark, in the
outset, that the cause is *not* to be found in the *original* nature of man.   Upon this point the evidence
is clear and strong.   As made, man was under Divine approval.*   This could not have been said if
his original constitution had been in any part, or in
any degree, corrupt, and a source of sin.   He possessed spiritual life.   As to his animal nature he
was, and is, made from the "dust of the ground."
But by whatever process formed, he "became a
living soul" by the Divine inbreathing of life.†
No doubt the expression, "breathed into his nostrils
the breath of life," means in its highest significance
something widely different from the filling of the
lungs with air.   It was rather the impartation of
that higher form of life—far above mere animal
or mere rational life—in virtue of which man could
hold direct spiritual communion with God,‡ please
Him in character and conduct,§ be justly regarded
as in the Divine image,*† and be, in another sense
than that which could be claimed for animals in

---

*Gen. 1, 31.   †Gen. 2, 7.   ‡Gen. 1, 28-30; 2, 16-17.   §Eccl. 7,
29.   *‡Gen. 1, 26; 5, 1.

general, a "son of God."* He was sound in body and in mind, infirmities and sicknesses being among the results of sin which were to be removed by that redemption which should restore man to Divine favor.† Here, then, was a being by every scriptural test free from sin, capable of continuing in holiness, and capable of begetting a sinless offspring And yet, "all men have sinned and come short of the glory of God."

---

*Luke. 3, 38. †Mat. 8, 17.

Students will find valuable discipline in preparing an outline of each chapter after having carefully read it. It will enable them not only to remember distinctly its leading points, but to get more from their subsequent reading. Something like the following is suggested :

Outline of Chapter II, "Universality of Sin."

    I.   Reasons for considering.
        1. To show Divine skill.
        2. To understand redemption.
    II. Affirmed.
    III. Proofs.
        1. Scriptural.
        2. Experimental.
    IV. Confessed.
        1. By Heathens.
        2. By Jews.
        3. By Christians.
    V. Remedy.
        1. Sought.
            1. In Philosophy.
            2. In Religion.
        2. Found.
            1. In Christianity only.
    VI. An added proof of universal sin among men.
    VII. A Question.
    VIII. Sin not in the original nature of man.

CHAPTER III.

CONSEQUENCES OF SIN.

" The wages of sin is death."—Rom. 6, 23.

SIN has its consequences—unhappy consequences of course. This goes without argument. It is written as a conviction in every heart, and exemplified in every life. Even the child who sins is conscious of remorse and a "certain fearful looking-for of judgment " in some sense or other.

But the consequences of sin are not all of one kind. Some of them are merely *physical.* The drunkard loses the power of muscular control, and becomes habitually unsteady. His face as well as his action, reveals his weakness, and you know him, at sight, a dissipated man. Doubtless every sin makes its mark upon the body. This thought seems to have been in the mind of the prophet Isaiah, in his vivid portrayal of the decadence of the Jewish nation : "From the sole of the foot even unto the head, there is no soundness in it."*

Sin has its *mental* consequences. The drunkard, glutton, sensualist, loses in greater or less de-

---

*Read Is. 1, 4-6.

gree the powers of memory, reasoning, imagination and will; and also becomes gross in his tastes and affections. He is merely a striking example. No doubt every sin injures mind as well as body.*

Sin has its *moral* consequences. It produces in most minds—probably in all—a peculiar suffering termed remorse, pain at having sinned, mingled with forebodings of the consequences. This is not all. The sinful indulgence of any appetite, desire or affection, creates or intensifies the disposition to such indulgence, and weakens the power to resist it. Not a sin so small but it reduces the moral nature to a lower level. This process may be carried on until one loses his power to appreciate the truth that would lead him to salvation, and deliberately prefers a life of sin to a life of holiness.†

It is a painful fact that these several consequences of sin, remorse excepted, are not confined to the person who commits the sin. By example and contact the sinner poisons his associates. By diminishing his power to do the noblest part toward others, sin makes him a robber. Sadder still, his weaknesses of body, mind and character, are transmitted to his posterity; for in this sense the iniquities of the father are visited upon the children.‡

*Titus 1, 15. †Math. 13, 15. ‡Ex. 20, 5.

Not a human being lives who does not suffer from the sins of associates and ancestors. By far the larger part of human suffering is the result of sin.

Mournful as are these, which may be called the *natural* consequences of sin, there is another which is yet more appalling, and that is the *legal* consequence. The just, wise, loving Creator, at once the Legislator, Judge and Executive over all his creatures, has attached a universal *penalty* to sin; and though he did not consult our preference, any more than an earthly judge would ask a criminal to choose his own sentence, he has very distinctly told us what the penalty of transgression is. "The wages of sin is death." "The soul that sinneth, it shall die."*

It is important that we know what is meant by these expressions. That "die" and "death," in these places, do not refer to the death of the body, is made very clear by numerous Scripture evidences, among which are the following: God said to Adam, "In the day that thou eatest thereof thou shalt surely die."† Yet Adam lived hundreds of years after his

---

*Ez. 18, 4, 20. For the reasons why this cannot now be included among the *natural* consequences of sin, see chap. V.
†Gen. 2, 17.

transgression. Physical death, then, could not have been intended, except, perhaps, as an outward evidence or a natural consequence of the real penalty. The terms " die," " dead " and " death " are frequently used, as in this case, to denote a spiritual, not a bodily state. Jesus said, " Let the dead bury their dead."* Here the word is evidently used once of spiritual and once of bodily death. " Ye were dead in trespasses and sins."† " Thou hast a name that thou livest and art dead."‡ "She that liveth in pleasure, is dead while she liveth."‖ " Hath passed from death unto life."§ " Shall save a soul from death."§§ " We know that we have passed from death unto life."†† " He that loveth not his brother abideth in death."††

The Bible clearly teaches the immortality of the soul in the sense of its everlasting duration.‖‖ The above passages have, therefore, no reference to the destruction or annihilation of the soul, or the loss of conscious existence. John, in speaking of this death in its final hopelessness says, " This is the second death," ¶ and figuratively describes it as being "cast into the lake of fire." Paul defines it

---

*Math. 8, 22. †Eph. 2, 1. ‡Rev. 3, 1. ‖1 Tim. 5, 6. §Jno. 5 24. §§Jas. 5, 20. ††1 Jno. 3, 14. ‖‖See Appendix D. P. 175. ‖Rev. 20, 14.

in its final form, as "everlasting destruction from the *presence of the Lord and from the glory of His power*."* Death does not mean, then, that the powers of thinking, feeling and willing are to cease ; but that the soul will be lost to those precious comforts, supports, incentives and means, which are necessary to regeneration and holiness and permanent happiness ; for these are found only in union and communion with God Himself. Even Cain seems to have had a very clear apprehension of the nature of the penalty for sin, as shown in his sad, though selfish complaint about his punishment, when he says to Jehovah, "From thy face shall I be hid."†

Although every consequence of sin to the sinner, may be regarded as subordinate to, as included in, or as issuing from its one specific penalty, yet the popular notion that physical death and that every sickness, accidental injury, or premature death—in short, every form of calamity or suffering —is a *penalty* for sin, and not, in general, a mere *natural consequence* of sin or of its penalty, is at once injurious and unscriptural. Nations, cities and armies have suffered from famine, pestilence, earthquake, fire and sword, as a special, visible pen-

---

*2 Thes. 1, 9.   †Gen. 4, 14.

alty for particular sins, or for extreme sinfulness. The destruction of the antediluvians by the flood,* of Sodom and Gomorrah by fire from heaven,† of Pharaoh and his hosts by the Red Sea,‡ of Korah and his company by earthquake and fire,§ of the hosts of Sennacherib by an angel of the Lord,** are all examples of suffering for flagrant sins. Examples of similar suffering by individuals, are seen in the ejection of Adam and Eve from Paradise,†† the sudden death of Nadab and Abihu,‡‡ the leprosy of Miriam§§ and of Gehazi,*† the agonizing death of Herod Agrippa,*‡ the blindness of Elymas the sorcerer,*§ the death of Ananias and Sapphira.*††

An examination of these cases will show that the suffering was not a natural consequence of transgression or sinfulness, but a direct visitation from God, to show His displeasure with sin, and His power to punish it.

But such cases are far from proving that all human suffering is penal. In the destruction of cities, nations and armies for sin, innocent persons, no doubt, often suffered, and those who were right-

---

*Gen. 6 and 7. †Gen. 19, 24-25. ‡Ex. 14, 24-28. §Num. 16, 31-35. **2 Ki. 19, 35. ††Gen. 3. ‡‡Lev. 10, 1-2. §§Num. 12, 10. *†2 Ki. 5. 27. *‡Acts 12, 23. *§Acts 13, 11. *††Acts 5, 1-10.

eous. The suffering of these could not have been penal. But even those special visitations which are most clearly penal, ought not to be confounded, in our minds, with the final and universal doom of the ungodly, which the Bible repeatedly calls "death," which Jesus calls "eternal punishment,"* "the condemnation of hell,"† "outer darkness,"‡ "the fire that never shall be quenched;"§ which Daniel calls "shame and everlasting contempt;"** and which Paul describes as "everlasting destruction from the presence of God and from the glory of His power."*†

No wonder that Christ and His apostles labored so earnestly to turn men from sin; for they distinguished clearly between that which is temporal and that which is eternal, and between all forms of suffering which may naturally result from one's own sin or that of another, and the one Divinely appointed, individual penalty for transgression. No wonder that Paul should exclaim, "Knowing therefore the terror of the Lord, we persuade men;"*‡ or that Peter should say, "I will not be negligent to put you in remembrance of these things, though ye know them."*§   And no wonder

---

*Mat. 25, 46.   †Mat. 23, 33.   ‡Mat. 8, 12.   §Mk. 9, 43, 45, 48.
  **Dan. 12, 2.   *†2 Thess. 1, 9.   *‡2 Cor. 5, 11.   *§2Pet. 1, 12.

that the awakened soul cries out, in view of such a doom, " What must I do to be saved ?"

It may help us to understand the meaning of death as the penalty of sin, the present state of the unsaved, and the final and fixed state of those who die [physically] in their sins,* to observe a few plain natural facts. We say of a man who is totally blind, and we may say it truly, without any figure of speech, that he is dead to the direct influences of light and color. They exert no power over his pursuits or his decisions, nor minister to his joy. Similarly, the man who is totally deaf, is dead to the power of harmony. Men are found who want some particular mental power, as that of number. Such a man is dead to the splendors and advantages of mathematics. Occasionally a person is found physically and rationally alive, yet morally well nigh dead; moral truth being apparently beyond his grasp, and moral principle having no power in his conduct. Just so, a man may be physically, mentally and morally alive, yet *spiritually dead*, as God declares every unpardoned sinner to be. Hence it is that " The natural man receiveth not the things of the Spirit of God, neither can he know them, because they are spiritually discerned."†

---

*For difference between this state here and hereafter, see Appendix A.   P. 157.   †1 Cor. 2, 14.

It is proper to note that the death here described involves the loss of those lofty and blessed
relations to God the Creator which are attributed to
man as at first created. The soul suffering this penalty no longer enjoys the Divine approval, whatever
be his outward conduct.*   He is no longer in direct
communion with God,† nor capable of any direct
knowledge of Him.‡   In spirit and purpose he is
contrary to God.§   He enjoys no longer in its truest, loftiest sense the Divine fatherhood, but is under that of the Adversary and Deceiver.**   He is
no longer in the Divine image.††   Nor is he capable of begetting a pure offspring.‡‡

Each of these statements the reader can fully
confirm by an examination of the accompanying
references, and by observing that the restoration of
man to *life* and to the lofty relations involved in it,
is the great *purpose* and *burden* of the Gospel.

---

*Eph. 2, 3.   †1 Cor. 2, 14.   ‡John 17, 3.   §Rom. 3, 9-19.   **John
8, 42, 44 ; 2 Cor. 6. 17-18.   ††Rom. 8, 29; 2 Cor. 3, 18 ; Col. 3,
10.   ‡‡A natural and necessary inference from what precedes;
but see also Ex. 20. 5.

CHAPTER IV.

IN ADAM ALL DIE.

"And so death passed upon all men, for that all have sinned."
—Rom. 5, 12.

THE positive statement of the inspired apostle that death passed upon all men, is but the logical conclusion from the premises contained in the headings of the two preceding chapters. "In Adam All Die."† The awful gloom in which our first parents passed out of Paradise, must have been deepened by the thought that it was to be the inheritance of their posterity. A fallen race! Rational indeed, but not spiritual; intelligent, but unloving and unbelieving; aspiring proudly, but not heavenward; "raging waves of the sea, foaming out their own shame, wandering stars, to whom is reserved the blackness of darkness forever."‡ *

Yesterday their souls had delighted in the splendors and harmonies of the universe. Their hearts had thrilled with "joy unspeakable and full

---

†1 Cor. 15, 22. ‡Jude. 13.

*The reader must bear in mind that the picture here drawn is that of fallen man, as he must have been, under the penalty of spiritual death, *had no provision been made for changing his state.* We shall see, later, in what respects this state *has* been changed by the suffering of Christ.

of glory ;" for they were in and of the kingdom of
God.   To-day they are translated into another kingdom—"sold under sin."   Their hearts are changed
toward God and good.   " All the foundations of the
earth are out of course."*   Eden itself is no longer
restful, beautiful, praise-inspiring.   No place shall
be so where God is, for they love Him no longer.
The only poor semblance of comfort they shall
know, will be when God is not in all their thoughts.

"So He drove out the man."† What a change!
Spiritual life is gone, but the rational soul remains,
a selfish, suffering witness of the stupendous transformation.   When the first clear knowledge of this
broke upon them, no doubt our first parents sent
up such a cry of anguish as earth should never witness again, save when the Sinless One should
descend to the same depth of suffering for their
redemption.

Mark the sad, sure decline of those whom God
made in His own image.‡   First—and upon the
plane of unsullied spiritual life—comes a bold
temptation.   God, in whom to them was the fulness of joy, had spoken; and loving obedience was
bliss. Satan speaks. It is a strange, opposing
voice : " Ye shall not surely die."§ The begin-

*Ps. 82, 5.   †Gen. 3, 24.   ‡Gen. 1, 27.   §Gen. 3, 4.

ning of consent is the listening ear; therefore take heed what ye hear. But might the strange voice of the Serpent be true? Might God's word be in some sense at fault? And with the indulgence of such thoughts, holiness, which then as now depended on unquestioning trust, was forfeited; a sinward tendency was implanted; desire was awakened; it heightened with contemplation, culminated in willful transgression, and man, the rebel, was an outcast.*

And *so* death passed upon all men? Shall we say it? By the logic of nature, yes; for the parent could not transmit to his children what he himself did not possess. The offspring of a beast is a beast, not a rational being. The spiritually dead could beget "a son in his own likeness,"† that was all. The state which came to Adam as the penalty of transgression, must therefore be entailed by natural law upon his posterity. They must belong to the kingdom of darkness and death, not to the Divine kingdom of light and life.

Would the infant, then, who is quite incapable of transgression, be included in this kingdom of darkness? How could it be otherwise? But has not God said of penal suffering, "The son shall

---

*John 15, 6. †Gen. 5, 3.

not bear the iniquity of the father?"* He has, and His word endureth forever. The state of darkness and separation from God will come to the child as hereditary diseases come, by the law of natural descent. It will be only his misfortune, not his fault. To the infant there is no law, for he cannot apprehend law; and "when there is no law, sin is not imputed."† His state by nature, though identical with that of his fallen parent, will not be to him a direct penalty, though he is clearly included in the condemnation of the race. Nor will it, though deplorable in the eyes of those who know a far better state, be attended with the poignancy of a direct penalty. The child has known no other state. A person born blind does not suffer like one who has become blind.

Yet in a state of natural blindness, having "fellowship with the unfruitful works of darkness," "hateful and hating one another," "having no fear of God before their eyes," "having no hope, and without God in the world,"‡ must Adam and

---

*Ez. 18, 20. †Rom. 5, 13.
‡For fuller interpretation of Ez. 18, 20, see Ch. xvii.

NOTE—Whatever be our views of the fatherhood of God (see Appendix F, page 191), we must not forget that so far as sin, its penalty, and the remission of its penalty are concerned, He stands in a *judicial* relation to us, as a righteous Sovereign; though in His fatherly character, lovingly providing for our restoration to His favor.

his posterity be, and in that state remain, as a consequence of Adam's transgression, unless God's love shall intervene to change in some way their state, by first changing their relation to His perfect law. Has there been such intervention ?

CHAPTER V.

DEAD THROUGH OUR TRESPASSES.

"And so death passed upon all men, for that all have sinned."
—Rom. 5, 12.

WE have not yet done with this text. We have seen how death must naturally have passed upon all men, in consequence of Adam's transgression, so that it might be truly said, " In Adam all die." Yet this is not stated in our text, where the reason assigned for death having passed upon all men is that " *all have sinned*."* This makes every man responsible for the state of death in which he is as a sinner, and makes that state a direct penalty, visited upon every man *for his own sin*. The question at the close of the preceding chapter, this text, therefore, answers clearly and affirmatively. There *has* been an intervention of Divine love to change, in some way, the state of the child.

This is evident for the following reasons: If every man has come under the penalty of death for his own sin, then before he committed sin he was not under the penalty. This must be true, there-

---

*For reasons already given, it is clear that this expression can not apply to infants, but to the accountable portion of the human family.

fore, of every child before he reaches the years of understanding. But was he not in a state of death as a natural consequence of Adam's penalty, though not suffering it as a direct penalty? This might be true but for one reason. If before the transgression the child were already in a state of death, it is clear that death could not afterwards be awarded him as a penalty for transgression, unless he were first made alive. If a murderer were sentenced to prison for life, he might again commit murder, but could not again receive the former punishment, unless the former sentence had been wholly or in part remitted. It is, therefore, a necessary inference from the text, that before the commission of conscious transgression every child possesses a kind of life which he could not inherit by natural law from our first ancestor, and which, upon willful transgression, he forfeits.

This thought seems to have been in the mind of the apostle Paul, when he said of himself; "For I was alive without the law once; but when the commandment came, sin revived and I died."* The remorse of a tender child upon the occasion of his first willful and deliberate disobedience has, no doubt, a significance far deeper than most persons

*Rom. 7, 9.

imagine. It marks the sad change from innocence to guilt, and the forfeiture of that life, which, more than any outward comforts, had made the rational life of the child a life of joy.

Take now the text which stands at the head of this chapter, and read it in connection with the one which precedes it in the Bible. " By one man sin entered into the world, and death by sin, and so death passed upon all men, for that all have sinned." We may now clearly see the meaning of the apostle to be: 1—That by Adam's transgression death entered into the world—came to Adam as a direct penalty, and to his race not as a direct penalty but a necessary consequence of *his* penalty. 2—That by some wonderful provision of grace, a measure of spiritual life is conferred upon every descendant of Adam, which elevates it to a state of personal accountability respecting its own final salvation. 3—That though the gravest consequence of Adam's penalty is thus removed, so that spiritual death is not entailed as a consequence of Adam's sin, yet the physical, mental and moral consequences of sin in the parent impart to the child such a *disposition or tendency* to sin, and the world furnishes him such *incentives* to sin, that those who reach the years of understanding do, without exception, transgress the Divine law; and 4—Because of this, their own transgression, they come under the same penalty which Adam suffered for his transgression.

When the apostle says to the Ephesians, " Ye were by nature the children of wrath, even as others,"* he might mean that, according to natural law, and without a special provision of grace, your state must have been that of spiritual death; or he might mean, though by grace ye were not, when children, in a state of death, yet your natural tendencies to sin were such that, like others, you yielded to temptation and came under Divine condemnation.

One of these interpretations would be as agreeable to the tenor of Scripture teaching as the other; but the latter was evidently in the apostle's mind, as shown by the subjoined statement that God, " even when we were dead *through our trespasses*, quickened us in Christ."†

In the considerations now presented, we find comfort and hope respecting irresponsible children. Yet we must wonder how the righteousness of God, by which the entire race was separated from Him, could, consistently with His attribute of unchang-

---

*Eph. 2, 3. †Eph. 2, 5.

ing justice, admit such a provision of grace. Prais-
ing him for the fact, we will leave the condition of
little children and their salvation, to resume it at a
proper time. The case of those who have forfeited
life and come under death for transgression, is to us
of greater moment.*

---

*It may be well here to note that the great truth brought to
view in this chapter, and more clearly explained in Chapter
XVII, seems to have been wholly overlooked by some who
have, therefore, taught that the present state of all persons
except the elect, is that of "total depravity," death, darkness, sinfulness ; and hence have inferred the condemnation
of many who die in infancy. See Appendix E, Total Depravity.

CHAPTER VI.

DIFFICULTIES OF THE PROBLEM.

"If our sins and our iniquities be upon us, and we pine away in them, how should we then live?"—Ez. 33, 10.

DARKENED, so that he cannot clearly perceive the truth; sinful, so that he willfully resists the truth; condemned so that he could not profit by the truth; the saddest feature in all this gloomy picture of fallen man, whether as a member of a condemned race, or as fallen by his own transgression, is his helplessness. *Dead* in sin. No wonder that a soul *brought* in any way to a *sense* of its awful state, should cry out, "How shall we then live?"

Let us observe particularly some of the considerations which must lead to this despairing question.

1—The punishment inflicted for sin *is just.* "Shall not the judge of all the earth do right?"* If just, the condemned cannot demand nor expect a remission of any part of their penalty. Inflexible justice must be an attribute of God as well as Infinite Love. Otherwise the universe must lose confidence in its Governor. "Hath He said and

*Gen. 18, 25.

shall He not do it? Or hath He spoken and shall He not make it good?"*

2—Under just sentence as rebels against God, we could have no course but to submit to our punishment. Every mouth is stopped. If the punishment is in any degree, or in any sense remitted, such remission must be a mere favor on the part of God, a free gift of His mercy. But Divine mercy cannot set aside Divine justice, nor work an abatement of it. If it should, it would make Divine justice appear to have been unjust; or else it would appear that God had changed his character or His purpose. In either case, the universe must lose confidence in its Governor. His government of moral beings certainly requires that He "change not;"† that He be "the same yesterday, to-day and forever;"‡ even if he could possibly be otherwise.

3—Even if God knows some way by which He may be just and remit our penalty, He cannot do so without working a most wonderful change in our natures; for we belong to an adverse kingdom, and our nature and all our incentives are opposed to Him. This, again, would be only a favor, nothing that we can claim or demand. Moreover, to change us will be impossible without our will; for

*Num. 23, 19. †Mal. 3, 6. ‡Heb. 13, 8.

the unchanging God has given us, as a fixed element of our nature, the powers of choice and volition.   We are in death because we chose sin with death, rather than obedience with life.   God will certainly demand, if He forgive us, a change in the bent of our free will.   He must, therefore, furnish us *incentives* to a change of will; for the kingdom of Satan does not furnish such incentives.   He must come to us on the plane of rational life, for spiritual life we have not.   He must bring light into our darkness, and must give us power to apprehend light.   To lead us to love Him, He must address Himself to our self-love.   To enable us to understand Him, He must speak through such things as we can understand.   We should need "a daysman between us, an interpreter," and he must speak with Divine authority.

4—But alas! this is not all.   Should God be able and willing to do all of this, the master to whom we have sold ourselves, will not let us go. He will present so many persuasions and threats, fill us so with doubt and fear, and with repugnance for God, that we shall never finally decide for Him. We must not only have had a measure of life to make a heavenward desire possible—a momentary lifting, at least, of our penalty; and a measure of

Divine light as a ground of instruction and hope ; but we must be assured of Divine help to detect the stratagems and overcome the efforts of our present sovereign and father, God's archenemy. We must have not only a daysman clothed with Divine authority, but a Captain clothed with Divine power. He must be God, that we may trust Him, and man that we may understand Him.

5—Yet more. He must afresh set before us God's righteous law ; he must give us the plainest assurance that *we* may keep it by God's enabling grace. He must therefore keep it himself, and that upon the plane of human infirmity and human environment.

6—And, finally, we must be assured that, after we have with full purpose of heart renounced the kingdom of Satan for that of God, our Judge—in case we are taken in sin by the sudden craft of the enemy, and so merit condemnation—will suspend the execution of His righteous law until it is clear that we purpose allegiance to another, or until we have become indifferent to the claims of God upon us.

Such being the weighty, and in the nature of the case the necessary conditions of our deliverance, "How should we then live?" Such must have been, in substance, the despairing thought of our first parents when driven out of Eden, and when the possibility of restoration had flashed upon them. The question, after reflection, could not have been, " What must I do to be saved ?" for evidently they could do nothing; but What can God do to save me ?   Before this question angels and men may well have stood perplexed.

The salvation of those who were under just condemnation, must perfectly vindicate Divine justice. At the same time it must furnish the sinner a plea. It must likewise give some experimental knowledge of the joys of *Life*, through which to impart some knowledge of Divine law, of sin and its consequences, of God's will to save, His power to save, and His way of salvation.   It must restore to perfect sonship, transform into the Divine image, bring into conscious communion with God, and into perfect harmony with His will.   It must remove all the consequences of sin, whether natural or penal ; and from the beginning of this process in any individual, it must cover perfectly his irresponsibility, and must also withhold penalty for committed sin until persistence in sin had made repentance impossible.

CHAPTER VII.

A DIVINE SUGGESTION.

"And He saw that there was no man, and he wondered that there was no intercessor ; therefore His own arm brought salvation."—Is. 59, 16.

IT is now our privilege to consider the wonderful manner in which Divine wisdom has met every one of the difficulties of human salvation without any abatement of Divine justice, and without destroying the freedom of the human will.   But let it be constantly borne in mind that in the character of Law-giver, Judge and Executive over all His intelligent creatures—a character in which He is constantly presented to us in the Scriptures, and in which we are necessarily bound to consider Him— God could not have been under any *obligation* to provide for man's salvation, whom he had justly condemned, and that His provision was, therefore, only an act of favor or love, issuing in infinite compassion.

It is clear that the most difficult feature of this intricate problem must be the lifting of the curse or penalty ; first as a race-penalty, so that it shall not be entailed, and then as a personal penalty from those who have incurred it by their own transgression. The transformation of character by the impartation of a new nature, must logically come after pardon and be conditioned upon it. Chronologically the two are, or appear to be, simultaneous.

If God were merely an arbitrary sovereign, He might bestow upon man an unconditional forgiveness. But this would be to raise the rebel to an equality with the loyal and trustworthy servant. If this shocks our common sense of justice, much more is it contrary to the absolute holiness of God. It would invade heaven with impurity. It would utterly destroy the moral government of the universe; for it would represent the Divine Being to His creatures as wanting in practical wisdom and love. This ought to be a sufficient answer to the impenitent sinner who says, "God made me, He is bound to save me."

The question may then be asked, Could not God bestow forgiveness—remission of penalty—upon such sinners as became truly repentant? This may look plausible, but a little thought will show it to be quite impossible. Like an unconditional forgiveness, it would set Divine mercy in opposition to Divine justice, as if, in the bosom of God these were contending rather than coincident and harmonious emotions.

The inferior kingdom, to which the soul is banished in penalty for transgression, could not furnish the needful incentives to repentance, nor any ground of hope that such repentance would be accepted by the Almighty. These must come, if they come at all, from God Himself. If we could conceive of true repentance and amendment of life as possible without a Divine intervention in behalf of the transgressor, even then, to offer pardon and life upon repentance would be a relaxation of Divine justice. But to offer these upon this condition, and then furnish gratuitously all the light and all the incentives necessary to such repentance, would be to acknowledge a lack of justice, wisdom or love in having made death the wages of sin. God cannot thus impeach, even by implication, His own perfections ; nor can man ask or expect of Him a procedure so contrary to all that makes Him an object of adoration and love.

How, then, *can* God be just and pardon the sinner, accept him to sonship and crown him with everlasting life ? Man could not have proposed a proper answer. Only God had either the right or the wisdom to suggest one. *He has done it.* He has placed before us a plan wholly unique, and adapted to meet every requirement of the case in the most perfect manner—a marvel of wisdom, power and love. It is *salvation by redemption*, nothing more; and the thought seems simple enough for the faith of a child. But it is redemption devised with such consummate wisdom, wrought out with such inimitable skill, and revealed to the race with such infinite tenderness, as must forever challenge the admiration of all worlds.

May God's blessing rest upon us in our effort to apprehend His plan; first in its *nature*, as displayed in God's own record of the race and of His Son, and attested by contemporaneous history uninspired; and then in its *relations* to the complex problem of human salvation, of which it is the masterly, because the Divine solution.

CHAPTER VIII.

THE SUGGESTION IN SHADOW.

" Without shedding of blood there is no remission."—Heb. 9. 22.

SCARCELY had the transgression of our first parents plunged them into the hopeless darkness of alienation from God, and deprived them of the unmeasured joys of Eden, when God revealed to them a door of escape from the kingdom and power of the Adversary. The references to this revelation in Genesis are scanty, contained in a few brief passages ; but evidences exist to show that in its essential features, the knowledge of the Divine plan of salvation, though afterwards obscured by the prevailing unbelief and sinfulness, was at first very clear and full.*

In the above text the apostle does not declare a new truth, nor one peculiar to Jewish thought. He merely states what had been believed from earliest times and probably in all nations. But the fact that it was a pervading principle of that wonderful law which was given to the Israelites through Moses, and that it is approvingly quoted and enlarged upon by the inspired apostle, sufficiently

*See Appendix H, "An Early Revelation." P. 199.

stamps it with the Divine approval. " No remission," that is, primarily, no removal or abatement of the penalty for sin, " without shedding of blood." The sacrificial systems of every nation and every age, attest most clearly that this singular truth was one of the first to appear in the human consciousness, and one which has commanded the confidence of devout men throughout the world's history. The cruel and foolish rites which crept into the religious systems of nearly all ancient peoples were merely human extravagances, which obscured but could not wholly conceal the matchless provision for human salvation.

Why no remission without blood? Because God's plan of redemption was redemption *by substitution*. Figuratively it was "eye for eye, tooth for tooth, hand for hand, foot for foot." Literally it was life for life, or more clearly death for death. If the spiritually dead is raised to life, it will be because another suffers the death penalty in his stead, and thus ransoms or redeems him from it. This is, in part, the thought which found expression in the ancient sacrifices with blood. It is the dominant thought in the Levitical law. It is the foundation of the Gospel of Jesus Christ.

In the light of the early, clear revelation of

God's purpose, Abel "brought of the firstlings of his flock, and of the fat thereof. And the Lord had respect to Abel and to his offering."* As he placed his hands upon the head of the lamb which he had brought, and with penitential tears confessed his transgressions ; as he acknowledged himself to be justly under pain of death, and besought the Lord for deliverance; as he proceeded to take the life of that choicest lamb, and asked God to accept the innocent for the guilty, and so to pardon his iniquity,† he exhibited that intelligent, obedient faith by which he "offered unto God a more excellent sacrifice than Cain."‡ That faith met its reward in a new heart, a changed life, the full assurance of hope, and blessed outward prosperity.

Cain was willing to make an offering to the Creator, but not an offering which would symbolize his own state, or God's chosen means for his redemption. His proud rejection of Divine authority, wisdom and love, hardened his evil heart, made him envious of his brother's joys, and resulted in bitter hatred and murder.

When Cain manifested displeasure that his offering was not accepted, the loving Divine answer indicates the reason for his rejection : " If thou

*Gen. 4. 4.   †Description taken from the Levitical law.
‡Heb. 11. 4.

doest well, shalt thou not be accepted ; and if thou doest not well, a sin offering coucheth at the door ; and its desire shall be to thee, but thou shalt rule over it."*

Later in the world's history, Noah was found righteous before God.† One family alone in all the world clinging to the blessed truth, the assertion of which had cost Abel his life. And when that family emerged from their long confinement in the ark, and descended to the plain, the genuine old " preacher of righteousness," as his first business, " builded an altar unto the Lord, and took of every clean beast and every clean fowl and offered burnt offerings on the altar."‡

Still later, Abraham offered, and taught his household to offer, sacrifices with blood ; and gave to his son Isaac on Mount Moriah that wonderful object lesson which taught him with unmistakable clearness the doctrine of redemption by substitution.§

Scarcely less striking is the history of Job, who was wont to offer burnt offerings according to the number of his sons ; for Job said, " It may be that my sons have sinned, and renounced God in their hearts."**

---

*Gen. 4. 7. See Commentaries of Clark and others on this verse. †Gen. 7. 1. ‡Gen. 8. 20. §Gen. 22. 1-14. **Job 1. 5.

In the same living faith and under the immediate command of God, Moses instituted the passover and other typical sacrifices of the ceremonial law. The sin-offering so regularly and solemnly sacrificed,* always denoted a consciousness of sin, a belief that the wages of sin is death, and that the remission of this awful penalty could take place only by the acceptance on God's part, of the death of an innocent victim, instead of the death which had been justly visited upon the sinner. The trespass offering, on the occasion of particular sins, denoted the same.

Let it be here noted, that these offerings were made by the eminently pious, by men who were in habitual or frequent communion with God, their sacrifices having His evident approval. Associate with these important facts the prominence given in the Mosaic law to sacrifices with blood, and the approving recognition of the same in the prophecies and in the New Testament, and there remains no doubt that redemption by substitution was God's plan of salvation. But we must look much farther into this mystery of grace, before we shall discover its intrinsic charm, its eternal, unquestionable fitness for its intended purpose.

*Lev. 4. 2, 6, 7. †The burnt offering and the peace offering denoted, respectively, as their leading thought, consecration and thanksgiving.

CHAPTER IX.

THE SHADOW NOT THE SUBSTANCE.

"It is not possible that the blood of bulls and goats should take away sin."—Heb. 10. 4.

IN view of what has just been said, here is a startling statement. It belongs by its date to the Christian dispensation. It affirms that the Jews and Gentiles who offered slain beasts* as an atonement for sin, did not experience a remission of the death penalty in virtue of such offerings.

Had the human race, then, during its first four thousand years, followed a delusion? Or, had God, who could not possibly accept the death of mere animals as a substitute for the spiritual death of a human being, or in other words as a redemption price for a lost soul, accepted the *spirit* in which these sacrifices were offered, and *so* pardoned the penitent transgressor? This is the view taken by some; but it is open to grave objections, as being illogical and unscriptural, unless we suppose the penitent to have presented his offering as an object-ive and positive expression of his own personal

---

*NOTE—"Bulls and goats" here denotes animals of every kind used as sacrifices.

faith in a means of redemption Divinely appointed, efficient, and of far greater value than any which human hands could offer.

Did the ancients possess such a faith? Did they perform these bloody rites with conscious reference to a greater truth which lay beyond? Let them speak for themselves. Isaiah (B. C. 760) represents Jehovah as saying, "I delight not in the blood of bullocks, or of lambs, or of he-goats."* Like expressions occur in several of the later prophetic books.† David much earlier (B. C. 1040), had said, "Burnt offering and sin offering hast thou not required."‡ Even Balak, a gentile king (B. C. 1450), cotemporary with Moses, despairingly exclaims, "Will the Lord be pleased with thousands of rams, or with ten thousand rivers of oil?"§ In most instances these and similar expressions may have had a local and temporary application; but they are also deeply significant of an enlightened consciousness on the great subject of human redemption.

Other expressions indicate the *reasons* why the death of animals could not have redemptive power. In the Psalms God is represented as saying, "I will

*Is. 1. 11. †Jer. 6. 20 and 7. 21-23; Amos 5. 21, 22, etc. ‡Ps. 40. 6. §Micah 6. 7.

take no bullock out of thy house, nor he-goats out of thy folds; for every beast of the forest is mine, and the cattle upon a thousand hills."* Men could not offer to God anything which was not already His own, and hence could not redeem themselves by sacrifice. Paul seems to have appealed with entire confidence to the men of Athens, when he said, "God is not worshiped with men's hands, as though He needed anything, seeing he giveth to all life, and breath, and all things;"† for wherever the idea of a Creator and Preserver of the world was entertained, there was also the thought that this same Creator must be the real possessor of that which He had made.

It is interesting to note in the records of the ancients, the numerous evidences of an uneasy longing for an offering that would be wholly satis-factory to the Almighty. When sacrifices are offered, they must be the *best* of the flock, *without blemish.*‡ Balaam required the king of Moab to build *seven* altars, "and he offered a bullock and a ram on every altar."§ The number seven, from very early times, denoted *completeness.* Here, then, the number of offerings stood for the fullness of repentance, consecration and faith; and expressed

---

*Ps. 50. 9, 10.   †Acts 17. 25.   ‡Lev. 22. 20.   §Num. 23. 2, 14, 30.

the longing for a perfect expiation. The seven offerings of Job for his sons, and the seven offerings of his three friends for their own folly,* have, doubtless, the same significance. The Jewish " daily sacrifice "† may have denoted the same longing, and the same restless, painful sense of the insufficiency of that which was offered. So may the *vast number* of offerings made by some of the ancient kings.‡

It is not uncommon to attribute whatever of clearness there is in relation to this subject in the Old Testament, to a sudden and immediate inspiration, under whose influence the prophets spoke better than they knew. Is it not more reasonable that most of their lofty and singularly harmonious teachings respecting the way of salvation were merely inspired utterances of beliefs common to those who lived in communion with God, among whom these beliefs were the subject of frequent conversation? There are strong reasons for answering this question in the affirmative. In the next chapter will be given a conclusive proof of a very early and wide-spread belief that " it is not possible that the blood of bulls and of goats should take away sin."

---

*Job 42. 8.   †Ex. 29. 38, 42.   ‡I. Ki. 8. 63; II. Chr. 15. 11.

CHAPTER X.

GOD MUST UNDERTAKE.

"None of them can by any means redeem his brother, nor give
to God a ransom for him."—Ps. 49. 7.

THE conviction of the devout men of ancient
times that the death of an animal could not
be accepted as an equivalent for the spiritual death
of a human being, is shown by the fact that it was
not accepted in atonement for murder, or as an
equivalent for *physical* death.* In that case nothing which a man possessed could be received in
expiation for his sin. But it is, if possible, more
clearly shown by the final resort to human sacrifices.
This was strictly forbidden by Jehovah, and was not
practiced by those who lived in communion with
Him ; but it was, and yet is, practiced by heathen
nations. That the purpose of these sacrifices, in the
minds of those who offered them, was immunity
from the just and ultimate penalty of sin, by substitution, is shown by the statements of heathen
writers, one of which it may be well to quote. It
is from Cæsar's commentaries on the Gallic war,
and is doubtless familiar to many. The writer
says (Book VI., chap. 16), "Every Gallic tribe is
much devoted to the practices of religion ; and

*Ex. 21. 12, 14; Lev. 24. 17.

hence those who are affected with severe diseases, and those who engage in battles or in dangers, either immolate human beings as victims, or offer themselves to be immolated, * * because they judge that they cannot reconcile the immortal gods unless for the life of a human being the life of a human being is given." This passage shows a recognition, even in the darkened heathen mind, of the Divine principle of substitution, and at the same time a belief of the insufficiency of animal sacrifices.

Turn now to the earnest inquiry of Balak, uttered fourteen centuries earlier, and observe how his thought rises to the suggestion of human sacrifices. "Wherewith shall I come before the Lord, and bow myself before the high God? Shall I come before Him with burnt offerings, with calves of a year old? Will the Lord be pleased with thousands of rams, or with ten thousands of rivers of oil? Shall I give my first-born for my transgression, the fruit of my body for the sin of my soul?"*

"Calves of a year old," though without blemish, he passes by as wholly insufficient. "Thousands of rams" would still be inadequate. What else can be thought of? His own cherished child,

---

*Micah. 6. 6, 7.

his "first-born." But even this the prophet passes by as insufficient, for he is speaking by Divine inspiration. He has heard proposed all that any man could propose. He sees that it is impossible for a man to procure his own redemption, or that of another; and he insists that the redemption must be provided by God Himself : for so we may interpret his answer : "God hath shown thee, O man, what is good; and what doth the Lord require of thee but to do justly and to love mercy, and to walk humbly with thy God."* As if he had said, Leave to God that which is beyond thy own wisdom and power, and which is the subject of His promise. How like this is Abraham's prophetic answer to Isaac, "God shall provide Himself a lamb, my son."

Substitution as the means of redemption, that was clear. A pure and innocent being alone could be accepted. To devout minds this was also clear. The blood of choicest beasts would not suffice : this again was clear. Nor yet the blood of one's own innocent "first-born." No man, however wealthy or powerful or holy, "can by any means redeem his brother," not even by dying in his stead. What then can be done? The provision must come from God. Only He can find a ransom.

*Micah 6. 8.

CHAPTER XI.

MEN AT THEIR WIT'S END.

"For the redemption of their soul is precious."—Ps. 49, 8.

THUS, in the light of Divine inspiration, reasoned the ancients. Accepting fully that " the wages of sin is death ;" " that all men have sinned," "and so death passed upon all men ;" that this death is not merely physical but spiritual death—" darkness," estrangement "from the presence of God and from the glory of His power ;" that salvation from such a state could come from God only, and only as a favor ; that to meet all the requirements of Divine justice, to preserve the moral government of the universe and the rights of all moral beings, God had ordained one means of salvation for fallen man, redemption by substitution ; accepting also that there could be no remission without shedding of blood, and that neither the blood of beasts nor that of man could be a redemption price for a lost soul, they looked to God alone to provide a sacrifice or offering which should have the necessary value.

Between a beast and even the most sinful man, was an immense difference—a difference not only in degree but in kind.   The sheep, ox or goat, had not a rational soul. Its wisest actions were scarcely so much as a mimicry of reason or conscience. Moreover, it had not illimitable duration.   Its existence ceased with its breath.   Its death agony was but physical and momentary.   How could the death of such a creature be accepted as an equivalent for the awful, enduring penalty for sin?   The redemption price must accord with the penalty in kind, and equal it in degree.*   The substitute must, therefore, be a rational, immortal being. Hence the intelligent, though misapplied, suggestion of a human sacrifice.

But this thought has its difficulties. Humanity might discover them, but could not rise above them. A sinner, though he should give his natural life for another, could not thus take the place of that other before the law—could not assume his penalty—because he is already under the same penalty.   He has no spiritual life to offer up that his fellow might be restored to spiritual life : and the offering of the natural life could not atone for sin, natural death not being the penalty for sin, but at the most only a consequence, or a minor part of that penalty.   A human being, to be accepted as an of-

*Is. 53. 4, 5.

fering, must have a spiritual life to offer, and must therefore be holy. Such and so precious must be the ransom of a soul. If such a one could give up his spiritual life, receiving in its stead the enduring sorrows of spiritual death that another might receive life, this and nothing less would truly vindicate Divine justice. True, the kingdom of Heaven would not gain a soul, except by the loss of one; because, from the nature of the penalty, one could not bear the penalties of two. Still for one this would be an equitable offering. But we are here met by three stubborn difficulties. 1— How could a redemption like this begin in a race every member of which was already in a state of death? For, apart from the Divine plan of redemption, this must have been the condition of every human being since the fall of Adam. And how could such a redemption be extended, if it were begun? 2—Again, if by some means or other a portion of the race were made holy, or had remained holy, and a holy man were offered for an unholy, he must be a voluntary offering; nay, more, he must lay down his own life, shed his own blood. Otherwise, the offering would be murder, and would prove the offerer criminal in the extreme and destitute of that humble repentance without which no offering could be accepted. 3—But further, God has put the offering of one human being for another out of the question, by so constituting man that the death of the body does not involve the death of the soul. Still less can it affect the spiritual life of a soul in possession of that life. The offering of a holy man for an unholy would hence be powerless as a ransom.

Evidently, Balak's question, " Shall I give my first-born for my transgression ?" and David's assertion, " None of them can by any means redeem his brother," mark the climax of human suggestion, and the despair of human effort respecting the all-important subject of human salvation.

CHAPTER XII.

ALL THE PROPHETS.

"What saith the Scripture?"—Rom. 4, 3.

MEANWHILE the Holy Ghost* was witnessing in every age† of a Divine provision yet to be made perfect, and directing the faith of the humble seeker after salvation to that provision.‡ To this refer God's statement in Genesis, that the seed of the woman should bruise the serpent's head;§ Enoch's vision, "Behold the Lord cometh with ten thousand of his saints;"** the prophecy of Abraham, "God shall provide Himself a lamb;"†† and Jacob's prophecy, "The scepter shall not depart from Judah, nor a lawgiver from between His feet, until Shiloh come, and to Him shall the gathering of the people be."‡‡

Of that coming Savior Balaam says, "I shall see Him but not now, I shall behold Him but not nigh;"§§ Job cries out joyously, "I know that my Redeemer liveth, and that He shall stand at the latter day upon the earth;"*† Moses says, "A prophet shall the Lord your God raise up unto you

---

*2 Pet. 1, 21. †Heb. 11. ‡Acts 10, 43. §Gen. 3, 15; Gal. 3, 16. **Jude. 14. ††Gen. 22, 8. ‡‡Gen. 49, 10. §§Num. 24, 17. *†Job 19, 25.

of your brethren, like unto me; Him shall ye hear in all things, whatsoever He shall say unto you; and it shall come to pass, that every soul which will not hear that prophet, shall be destroyed from among the people."* "To Him give all the prophets witness, that through His name whosoever believeth on Him shall receive remission of sins."†

Prophecy sets forth clearly that this Redeemer is GOD.‡ Not only is it true that no other can redeem us from the penalty of sin, but God Himself *will* do it. The provision made will have, therefore, an infinite value in it. One can "trust and not be afraid," if the Lord Jehovah is become his salvation.§ Whatever conditions the sinner may be required to fulfill on his part,** he can perform with the most perfect confidence; for a Divine Redeemer will be "able to save to the uttermost."††

But prophecy also clearly attributes to this wonderful Redeemer a *human* nature: "The seed of Abraham;"‡‡ "A man of sorrows and acquainted with grief;§§ "Numbered with the transgressors."*†

And prophecy declares Him to be God *and* man, in mysterious and wonderful union. "A virgin shall conceive and bear a son, and shall call His

*Acts 3. 22. †Acts 10. 43. ‡Ps. 19. 14; 78. 35; Is. 41. 14; 43. 14; etc. §Is. 12. 2. **Acts 20. 21. ††Heb. 7. 25. ‡‡Gen. 26. 4, etc. §§Is. 53. 3. *†Is. 53. 12.

name Immanuel,"* (God with us). "Unto us a child is born, unto us a son is given ; and the government shall be upon his shoulder ; and his name shall be called Wonderful, Counselor, The Mighty God, The Everlasting Father, The Prince of Peace."† "The Holy Ghost shall come upon thee, and the power of the Highest shall overshadow thee ; therefore that holy thing that shall be born of thee, shall be called The Son of God."‡ Thus "God sent forth His Son, made of a woman, made under the law, to redeem them that were under the law, that we might receive the adoption of sons."§

In this Son of God, Jesus Christ of Nazareth, center all the prophecies and allusions of the Old Testament, respecting a Redeemer, a Savior, a Deliverer, a Messiah, at once God and man. To Him point all the types of the law respecting atonement, propitiation, substitution, forgiveness, cleansing, salvation, life from the dead. In Him are fulfilled all those wonderful conceptions of character and conduct which had found expression in the law and in the writings of holy men of old, and a partial —never a complete—exemplification in good men's lives.

---

*Is. 7. 14.   †Is. 9. 6.   ‡Lu. 1. 35.   §Gal. 4. 4, 5.   See App. F. on Divine Fatherhood.

The character of Jesus is a perfect model. No philosopher or poet, however holy his life or however lofty his conceptions, has been able to suggest an improvement or shall be; for Jesus of Nazareth was God "manifest in the flesh."* By Him the devout inquirer may learn precisely what God would do if He were a man; for he may learn precisely *what God did* in the form and character and limitations of manhood.† It is therefore eminently proper to take Jesus as our pattern in character and conduct. But it should be remembered that no imitation of Christ can constitute salvation. The closest imitation of life is not life. "I am come that they might have life."‡

The moral teachings of Jesus are without a parallel. "Never man spake like this man."§ No man can add to His teachings or take from them without reducing their value. The doctrines propounded by Christ should therefore be reverently studied by every seeker after righteousness and every well-wisher of humanity. But alas! the unsaved can follow such teachings in the letter only —not in the spirit. Death cannot apprehend life. To the natural man the things of the Spirit of God are foolishness, "neither can he know them, because

*I. Tim. 3. 16.   †Phil. 2. 7.   ‡Jno. 10. 10.   §John 7. 46.

they are spiritually discerned."* To appreciate or practice those sublime precepts except in their rudiments and in a formal manner, one must first be conformed to the image of the Son by the impartation of a kindred *life* or *nature*.

The example and the teachings of Jesus perfectly corroborate and supplement each other. The study of both is indispensable to a Christ-like perfection. But intense study of these models and an earnest effort to exemplify them, may take place in one whose secret heart rebels against the fundamental requisition of God for salvation; even more, it may take place *because* the heart so rebels, and seeks this very imitation as a substitute for the Divine requirement. The resulting imitation is beautiful perhaps in many respects, but hopelessly deficient in the most essential particular. Nothing truly resembles life but life. A painter admires a stately maple, and puts it on canvas. The form and colorings seem exquisitely perfect. But out by the pathway is a slender maple twig, brushed and scarred by those who pass. Which of the two, the twig or the picture, most resembles the tree which evoked the artist's admiration? Not the picture, certainly, for in it there is not the possibility of the

---

*1 Cor. 2. 14.

leafage, fruitage, and dimensions of its stately original; while in the twig are all of these; for it has
life, and the *same kind* of life.

Now suppose that this painter wished that, instead of producing something that looked like a
tree, he himself might *be* like that tree. He would
see that between him and it there is a great gulf
fixed. It would certainly require a miracle to
change his life to its life, and impart to him the
power of unfolding its perfections, albeit those perfections are far inferior to his own. Still more,
then, must the natural man who would be like
Christ, undergo the miracle of transformation, "be
born from above." "If any man be in Christ, he
is *a new creature.*"* "Not new works done," said
Luther, "but a new man to do them;" for Luther
had caught the key-note of the gospel, which is
regeneration. "Ye must be born again."†

[When John says, "He that doeth righteousness is righteous,"‡ he is not asserting that doing
righteousness makes one righteous, but that righteousness is done only by him who is righteous; a
statement in harmony with that of the preceding
verse, "Whosoever abideth in Him sinneth not."§]

To see how the infinite Christ has provided for

---

*2 Cor. 5. 17. †John 3. 7. ‡1 John 3. 7. §1 John 3. 6.

this singular and amazing transformation; how he becomes to us not only a pattern and a lawgiver, but an actual Savior; how he saves us not only from possible sins, but from the penalty of committed sins; how he brings us from darkness to light, from the power of Satan unto God,* *from death to life*, is the object of our inquiry.

Lord, as we reverently seek to descend to the depths of this mystery—not as hidden among thy secret things, but as it has pleased thee to reveal it in the record of thy Son—sustain and direct us, that we may "show forth the praises of Him who hath called [us] out of darkness into His marvelous light."

---

*Acts 26. 18.

CHAPTER XIII.

CLEAR LIGHT ON THE PROBLEM.

"We see Jesus, who was made a little lower than the angels for
the suffering of death, crowned with glory and honor, that
He by the grace of God should taste death for every man."

—Heb. 2. 9.

WE are nearing the solution of the great problem of the ages. The death penalty under which the responsible but unbelieving portion of the human race are groaning, was inflicted
by God. It was therefore absolutely just. It will
therefore never be revoked. It may be—it will be
—borne by another. The Just will suffer for the
unjust, that the suffering may have redemptive
value. The Infinite will suffer for the finite, that
the suffering may be " for the whole world."*

The Son of God, in His regal state, could not suffer death. Satan had fallen from heaven ; and in
all its wide domain there lingered not one to whom
it could occur to condemn the Just, or utter one
word against Jehovah. Should the Son descend to
the estate of holy angels, even here would be perfect safety ; for they are in such harmony with
God, that they do always behold the face of the

*1 Jno. 2. 2.

Father. To be our Redeemer, then, the Son must leave the glory which He had with the Father before the world was, and present Himself in this world of sin, temptation, suffering and death. He was therefore " made in the likeness of men,"* " a little lower than the angels." This, however, was not the only reason why Christ came to earth. The earth was the abode of the race which He came to redeem. It was essential that He teach that race how to live acceptably to God, and that, in fashion as a man, He keep perfectly the Divine law, to prove to them that it *may* be kept. His coming was, therefore, essential to a perfect mediation. Upon the sin-cursed earth, where already holy men had sealed their testimony with their blood,† and wicked men had offered insult to angels,‡ Jehovah Himself appears for the suffering of death.§ Miracle of miracles! What a change! Incomprehensible yet real! The crowning wonder of the universe! The one hope of a fallen world!

Some persons have suggested that the incarnation would have taken place if sin had not entered into the world. Such a suggestion seems to be wholly gratuitous, and quite opposed to the plain

---

*Phil. 2. 7.   †Heb. 11. 37.   ‡Gen. 19. §See Appendix I, **Divine Passibility.**

teachings of the Scriptures. " Ye know that He was manifested to take away our sins."* " For this purpose the Son of God was manifested, that He might destroy the works of the devil."† " Now once in the end of the world hath He appeared, to put away sin by the sacrifice of Himself."‡ " Jesus Christ came into the world to save sinners."§

The perfect life and the inimitable precepts of Jesus were to be of inestimable value in persuading men to seek life eternal. They were also to be a mighty power for the unfolding of that life when obtained. But it required the *death* of Jesus *to procure* that life, or the possibility of it, to any member of our fallen race.

" Christ *died* for the ungodly."*† " God commendeth His love toward us in that while we were yet sinners, Christ *died* for us."*‡ " We were reconciled to God by the *death* of His Son."*§ " Ye were . redeemed . . . by the *precious blood* of Christ."** " Christ our passover is *sacrificed* for us."†† " This is my *blood of the new testament*, which is *shed* for many for the remission of sins."‡‡ Thus, and in various other ways, do the Holy Scriptures declare, that *not without the*

*1 Jno. 3. 5. †1 Jno. 3. 8. ‡Heb. 9. 26. §1 Tim. 1. 15.
*†Rom. 5. 6. *‡Rom. 5. 8. *§Rom. 5. 10. **1 Pet. 1. 18, 19.
††1 Cor. 5. 7. ‡‡Mat. 26. 28.

death of Christ for us can we hope for forgiveness and salvation.

The death of Jesus Christ was not, in its true significance, the death of a martyr. Even if the narrative indicates that the death was inflicted for certain utterances which Jesus refused to retract, still it is distinguished in the plainest possible manner from mere martyrdom.

1—The *language* used of Jesus' death, is nowhere used of the death of martyrs. The Bible speaks often of holy men who were put to death by their unbelieving brethren; but it nowhere says that they—not even the whole army of them—died *for* the ungodly; that "we were *reconciled to God*" by their death; that we "*were redeemed*" by their "*precious* blood;" that they were "our *passover, sacrificed* for us;" that their blood is the "blood *of the New Covenant*;" or that their blood was "*shed for the remission of sins.*" Yet these and numerous expressions of like import are applied to the death of Jesus Christ.

Our Savior Himself did not speak of His life as that of a mere teacher and exemplar, nor of His death as that of a martyr. "I give unto them eternal life; and they shall never perish, neither shall any man pluck them out of my hand."*   " I am the living bread which came down from heaven; if any man eat of this bread, he shall live forever; and the bread that I will give, is my flesh, which I will give for the life of the world."†   " My flesh is meat indeed, and my blood is drink indeed."‡ What man, however holy his life, however exalted his teachings, however courageous his spirit in anticipation of dying for the truth, has ever dared to utter words like these?   If Jesus Christ is entitled to our confidence as a moral teacher and character-pattern, we must expect Him to utter nothing beyond the truth when speaking of Himself. Yet His own testimony, like that of the prophets and apostles, exalts the purpose and value of His death above that of a mere martyr as far as the heavens are higher than the earth.

2—The *behavior* of Jesus also attests that He was not a mere martyr.   Why the awful agony in the garden?   Why the "sweat as it were great drops of blood falling down to the ground?"§ Why does he faint beneath the weight of His cross? Why does he not meet death with the triumphant gladness of Paul, or the trustful fortitude of Polycarp, or at least with the stoical composure of Soc-

*John 10. 28.   †John 6. 51.   ‡John 6. 55.   §Lu. 22. 44.

rates? The answer is plain, and no other answer meets the case at all. His was not the dread of mere physical death; for then he would have invalidated His own sublime maxim: "Be not afraid of them that kill the body, and after that have no more that they can do."* He was troubled in spirit† in anticipation and foretaste of the deeper, darker anguish of that hour in which His *soul* should be made an offering for sin ;‡ in which He should thus suffer as the innocent, voluntary, Divine victim, "*the Lamb of God*," whose death alone could effect the redemption of lost souls.

Jesus alone had the honor of being able and willing to suffer for our sakes an agony of spirit which humanity can but feebly portray or imagine; which, indeed, no human being can ever suffer in like degree nor for a like purpose, though the finally impenitent must suffer it in kind. Only the infinite Christ could and did " taste death for every man." " Wherefore God hath highly exalted Him, and given him a name that is above every name ; that at the name of Jesus every knee should bow, of things in heaven, and of things in earth, and of things under the earth; and that every tongue should confess that he is Lord, to the glory

---

*Lu. 12. 4. †Jno. 12. 27; 13. 21. ‡Is. 53. 10.

of God the Father."* The precise nature of that suffering, and something of its intensity and its value, we shall learn as we pursue the record.

---

*Phil. 2. 9-11.

CHAPTER XIV.

THE PREPARATION.

"This is your hour and the power of darkness."—Lu. 22. 53.

NOTHING more clearly attests the depravity of the human race, than its hostility to the pure and perfect Jesus of Nazareth. In the nation which had given to the world its most exalted conceptions of God and of man, of religion and of morality,* the Savior of men, God manifest in the flesh, is *mocked*, SCOURGED, CRUCIFIED, at the demand of the *chief priests and elders and scribes.*†

"*Had they known*, they would not have crucified the Lord of glory."‡ But why did they not know? They had the light of history, and prophecy, and experience, and should have passed every other nation and every preceding age in the wisdom that comes from the fear of the Lord. Yet, with means of enlightenment then unknown to any other generation or people, " this people's heart is waxed gross, and their ears are dull of hearing, and their eyes they have closed; lest at any time they should see with their eyes, and hear with their ears, and should understand with their hearts, and should be

---

*Ps. 147. 20; Rom. 3. 1, 2; Deut. 4. 32-37. †Mark 14. 43; Mat. 26. 59. ‡1 Cor. 2. 8.

converted, and I should heal them."* *They might have known.* Ignorance, so far from excusing them, was the crowning proof of their crowning sinfulness. And therefore " the Holy One and the Just " could say, " That upon you may come all the righteous blood shed upon the earth, from the blood of righteous Abel to the blood of Zacharias."† " How often would I have gathered thy children together * * but ye would not."‡

They were now prepared to deny the Holy One. They had become the fit instruments of Satan for enacting the most dark and cruel of tragedies. " Hereafter I will not talk much with you," said Jesus to His disciples, " for the prince of this world cometh, and hath nothing in me."§ On a former occasion He had said to the Jewish leaders, " Ye are of your father the devil, and the lusts of your father ye will do."** That word was about to receive fullest confirmation.

At the last supper, " the Passover, a feast of the Jews," Jesus exclaimed to His chosen twelve, " One of you shall betray me."†† Sad and wonderstricken, each asks the question, " Lord, is it I ?"‡‡ Jesus replies, " He it is to whom I shall give the sop when I have dipped it. And He gave it to Judas Isca-

---

*Mat. 13. 15. †Mat. 23. 35. ‡Mat. 23. 37. §Jno. 14. 30. **Jno. 8. 44. ††Mat. 26. 21. ‡‡Mk. 14. 19.

riot."* "And after the sop Satan entered into
him."† Judas at this moment yields his last
scruple, consents fully to the dark purpose which
had hitherto haunted him only as a temptation, and
the adversary takes full possession of his powers.
Presently, he shall see what he has done, and in an
agony of horror go out and hang himself; but at
this hour his mind is filled with plausible excuses
for the awful crime of betraying the innocent
blood.

He bargains away his Lord for thirty pieces of
silver.‡ He plans the capture.§ He leads "a
great multitude with swords and staves from the
chief priests and the scribes and the elders."** In
the garden of Gethsemane, hallowed by many an
hour of sweetest intercourse between Jesus and His
followers,†† the malignant crowd attempt to arrest
the sinless One. As He spake to them, such a power
came over them that they "went backward and
fell to the ground."‡‡ But this is their hour. Again
they rally and make Him their prisoner. They
have chosen the night, for they feared the people.§§
Even in this extremely literal sense, they are acting
under the power of darkness. Their enormous guilt
shuns the light. Even the council must convene

---

*Jno. 13. 26. †Jno. 13. 27 ‡Mat. 26. 14. §Mat. 26. 16. **Mk.
14. 43. ††Jno. 18. 2. ‡‡Jno. 18. 6. §§Lu. 22. 6.

in the night-time. The decision reached will not be legally binding, but it can be easily ratified after sunrise.* False witnesses appear, but there is no agreement in their testimony.† "At the last came two false witnesses and said, This fellow said, I am able to destroy the temple of God, and to build it in three days."‡ There was nothing in such testimony to prove a man a criminal. No wonder that "Jesus held His peace." Baffled, the High Priest puts a significant question: "Art thou the Christ, the Son of the Blessed?" "And Jesus said, I am; and ye shall see the Son of Man sitting on the right hand of power, and coming in the clouds of heaven. Then the High Priest rent his clothes, and saith, What need we any further witness? Ye have heard the blasphemy; what think ye? And they all condemned Him to be guilty of death."§ Such was the trial. "And some began to spit upon Him, and to cover His face, and to buffet Him, and to say unto Him, Prophesy: and the servants did strike Him with the palms of their hands."**

He is sent to Pilate. The Roman governor tries again and again to release Him. "I find no fault in Him." But the clamor of Jewish malice prevails. Washing his hands before them all, and

---

*Lu 22. 66.   †Mk. 14. 56.   ‡Mat. 26. 61.   §Mk. 14. 61-64.
**Mk. 14. 65.

exclaiming, "I am innocent of the blood of this just person,"* the heathen ruler nevertheless gives sentence "that it should be as they required."† Jesus then having endured the scourging, the smiting, the spitting, the vulgar mockery, is led forth TO BE CRUCIFIED. As if to link His name with infamy, two criminals are crucified with Him. The soldiers mock His thirst with vinegar; and the priests revile Him, wagging their heads. "He saved others," they say, "Himself He cannot save." "If thou be the Son of God, come down from the cross." "Thou that destroyest the temple and buildest it in three days, save thyself." Even the poor thief who hangs beside Him, joins in the expression of scorn.

Yet this is Jesus, the teacher and prophet, who for three years has exposed Himself to hardship and peril and incessant toil, for the sole purpose of bringing good to men. Monstrous cruelty! No reasoning can palliate it. "We will not have this man to reign over us." They knew that He was a teacher come from God;‡ yet through envy they delivered Him.§

Why did not Divine Love protect the innocent? Because sin was now to appear in all its hideousness; human nature in all its vileness. The vivid

---

*Mat. 27. 24. †Lu. 23. 24. ‡John 3. 2. §Mat. 27. 18.

contrast between this wanton outrage upon the person of Jesus, and the transparent purity of Jesus' life and work, will do much to make sin an object of hatred to all considerate beings. It must also refine and exalt the human conception of patience, forbearance, forgiveness—in short, of every one of those graces which shone so radiant in the life of the Savior. It must also furnish to the world the model of true heroism, and a true martyr spirit. Any of these three reasons might, perhaps, have been sufficient to prevent the Father from withholding His Son from the trial and the cross. But none of them, nor all of them, constitute *the* reason why Jesus was allowed to suffer.

God sent His Son into the world, "that the world through Him might be SAVED."* We could be *reconciled to God* only by the DEATH of His Son.† Jesus, who was as truly God as the Father, said in view of His coming agony, "Now is my soul troubled; and what shall I say? Father, save me from this hour? but for this cause came I unto this hour."‡ He had come to earth "*for* the suffering of death,"§ "that through death He might destroy him that had the power of death."** He had been announced by John, the forerunner, as "the Lamb

---

*Jno. 3. 17. †Rom. 5. 10. ‡Jno. 12. 27. §Heb. 2. 9. **Heb. 2. 14.

of God,"* which meant nothing less than that **He**
should "taste death for every man;"† die for all
because all were dead;‡ justify many by bearing
their iniquities § (that is, the penalty for their
iniquities); suffer, "the Just for the unjust, that He
might bring us to God;"** purchase us "with His
own blood;†† "redeem us from all iniquity"‡‡ "by
the sacrifice of Himself;§§ be the Divinely appointed "propitiation for our sins."*†

How strangely in this trying hour does the
character of Jesus contrast with the pride, the corruption, the malignity of fallen man—the light of
heaven with the darkness of hell! What loving
condescension that the Holy One should consent to
be made a little lower than the angels! What
astonishing condescension to suffer condemnation,
insult and crucifixion at the hands of sinful men,
that He might bring them to God! But the value
of the offering of Jesus lies *beyond all this*, in an
agony whose cause is hid from outward vision, and
which marks a condescension infinite beyond expression.

---

*Jno. 1. 29. †Heb. 2. 9. ‡2 Cor. 5. 14. §Is. 53. 11. **1 Pet.
3. 18. ††Acts 20. 28. ‡‡Titus 2. 14. §§Heb. 9. 26.*†1 Jno. 2. 2.

CHAPTER XV.

THE PERFECT SOLUTION.

"My God, my God, why hast thou forsaken me?"—Mat. 27. 46.

MOST persons seem to regard the physical death of our Savior as the direct result of the intense sufferings of crucifixion, and the loss of blood occasioned by His wounds ; and many, if not most, seem to regard His physical death as the atonement for our sins. These views, however, fall very far short of the truth.

Great as the agony of crucifixion must have been, those who suffered in this way lived for many hours, not unfrequently for two or three days, and in some instances, it is said, for more than an entire week. The Savior's death, however, occurred within a comparatively very short period, no estimate making it more than about six hours. The loss of blood from His nail wounds was probably not great, and His side was not pierced until after He was dead. " Pilate marvelled if He were already dead;"* "and when he knew it of the centurion, he gave the body to Joseph."† Again, the physical energy of Jesus' last utterances, clearly shows that His

*Mk. 15. 44.   †Mk. 15. 45.

death did not result from exhaustion. He " cried
with a loud voice."* We must look then, for some
other and unusual cause of death.

Upon this point the Bible has not left us without very clear evidences. We may first note the
peculiar form of Jesus own prophecies respecting
the death He was about to die. " The good Shepherd giveth His life for the sheep."† Not merely
risketh, but "*giveth*." " I lay down my life for the
sheep."‡ This might mean that Jesus would pursue a course that would lead to His crucifixion, but
it suggests also the death as directly dependent upon Himself rather than upon His murderers. " I
lay down my life, that I might take it again. No
man taketh it from me, but I lay it down of myself.
I have power to lay it down and I have power to
take it again."§ This statement of the voluntary
character of His death, may have been adequately
fulfilled by His allowing Himself to fall into the
hands of "betrayers and murderers." But it seems
to mean much more than this. " No man;" not
the chief priests, elders and scribes ; not Herod nor
Pilate ; not the soldiers who crucified Him ; " no
man."

Again, the death of Jesus was, from His own

*Mat. 27. 46, 50; Mk. 15. 37; Lu. 23. 46. †Jno. 10. 11.
‡Jno. 10. 15. §Jno. 10. 17, 18.

stand-point, the death of a sacrifice; Jesus, Him-self being the High Priest who offered it. " He offered up Himself."* It does not comport with the solemn dignity of His mission that the sacri-ficial death which was to atone for sin, should be inflicted by the malice of corrupt men. These were, to all intents, murderers, chiefly because sin lies in the intention. But as the High Priest who offered the legal sacrifices for the sins of the people must be anointed and holy, so Jesus, the great Antitype of those sacrifices, must be offered by one who was holy.

What, then, was the immediate cause of His death ? In the Garden His agony had been so great that " His sweat was, as it were, great drops of blood falling down to the ground."† Persons have sometimes been known to give similar evi-dence of extreme mental suffering ; but in all such cases the physical life is in danger. To Jesus, death must have seemed imminent. No nail had yet pierced Him ; no scourge had been laid upon Him. He had not been delivered to the Gentiles, nor had He suffered arrest. Should He die here in the Garden, His death might as perfectly atone for sin as if it transpired elsewhere. But then several of

*Heb. 7. 27.   †Lu. 22. 44.

His own prophecies would be unfulfilled, and some of the ancient ones also; and hence His atonement could not appeal as effectively to the faith of men. It is believed by many, that this thought prompted His thrice repeated prayer, "O my Father, if it be possible, let this cup pass from me; nevertheless not as I will, but as thou wilt."* The cup, not of death, but of premature death; death under circumstances which would render it so difficult of explanation, and deprive it, by so much, of its intended value, because interposing barriers to faith. Such an interpretation of Jesus' prayer seems to be justified by the remarkable statement of the apostle respecting our Savior, "Who," he says, "in the days of His flesh, having offered up prayers and supplications with strong crying and tears, unto Him who was able to save Him from death, and *having been heard* for His godly fear," etc.† To die upon the cross as a malefactor would be a bitter cup. But to Him who could say, "My meat is to do the will of Him that sent me, and to finish His work,"‡ death in the retirement of the Garden would be a cup more bitter, because not perfectly fulfilling the Father's declared will. "And there appeared unto Him an angel from heaven,

---

*Mat. 26. 39, 42, 44.   †Heb. 5. 7.   ‡Jno. 4. 34.

strengthening Him."* Under the limitations to which He had submitted Himself in order to become our Mediator, High Priest and Sacrifice, He who had upheld all things by the word of his power† could now need and receive strength from the Father, through the ministry of an angel.

With physical energy thus renewed, Jesus goes forth to accomplish all that was written and unfulfilled of His expiatory suffering; to witness the fulfilment of His own words respecting the betrayal, the mockery, the trial, the condemnation, the desertion and the crucifixion. " Heaven and earth shall pass away, but my word shall not pass away."‡

When all these particulars had been accomp-

---

*Lu. 22. 43. Many commentators, probably most of them, have supposed that the prayer, " Let this cup pass from me," had reference, not to the Gethsemane suffering but to the crucifixion itself. They hold that Jesus asked to be delivered from it if it were "possible," but was *not* so delivered because it was *not* possible to fulfill His mission in any other way for the salvation of men. I believe, with them, that no other way of salvation was possible ; but I believe also that the Savior *knew* this ; that He had once definitely said that He could not ask to be saved from it, and that He did not now ask it. The interpretation I have given is adopted by many, and seems to me the most consistent with other Scripture. That Christ's death was the only possible means of our redemption, is sufficiently proved by other evidence.

†Heb. 1. 3.   ‡Mat. 24. 35.

lished—then, and not till then—the great High
Priest offered up Himself. Then, and not till then,
did He descend to that depth of soul agony, which
the body could not possibly sustain, which he did
not seek to escape, and from which even the minis·
tration of angels would be withheld, because His
hour had come.   He will now "pour out His soul
unto death."*

"He is despised and rejected of men."†   Is not
this enough of humiliation?   He endures the tor-
ture of the cross.   Is not this enough of suffering?
Sympathy says, Yes; but truth says, No.   Type
and prophecy answer, No.   The awakened soul,
longing for eternal life, says, No.   Divine love in
the bosom of the Father and the Son, says, No.
Compared with the suffering which atoned for sin,
all the pains of scourging, desertion and crucifixion,
were only as the eddying gust to the destroying
whirlwind; as the ripple on the quiet lake to the
fury of angry surges.

Martyrdom is painful when, beyond the circle
of his tormentors, the sufferer can behold the faces
of sympathizing friends, and catch their words of
cheer, and their prayers for his support.   It is more
painful when friends have fled, or fear to utter

*Is. 53. 12.   †Is. 53. 3.

prayers or the promises of Divine comfort. Yet even in this extremity martyrs have sung and rejoiced, *because God was with them*, and the comforts of His love triumphed over physical suffering. But what if this comfort were denied them? How must all means of expression fail to portray their anguish.

Men who have resisted the earnest pleadings of the Holy Spirit, have writhed in anguish when they felt that that Spirit had forever departed. What if He withdraw His presence from the saint who has loved and trusted Him? To such a one the very thought is appalling. What must it have been to the only-begotten Son of God,* who had shared from everlasting the delights of the Father's house,† who did always the things that pleased Him‡ whose holiness was absolute, and whose love was infinite? Yet Jesus suffered all this. Not only did the sorrows of [physical] death compass Him, but the pains of *hell* gat hold upon Him.§ The Father's face is hid; and Jesus utters that piercing wail of anguish, "My God, my God, why hast thou forsaken me?" He does not say Father; for all the joy denoted by that fond word so often

---

*Jno. 3. 16. †Jno. 1. 1, 2. ‡Jno. 8. 29. §Ps. 86. 13; 116. 3.

on His lips, has given way to an overwhelming
sense of alienation and desertion.

Hide thy face, O Sun, from such a scene as
this! And thou, O Earth, if thou shouldst tremble
at the presence of the Lord, how shouldst thou now
quake, when He who has upheld thee by the word
of His power, descends to this awful extremity of
suffering? And thou, O sinful man, what shall I
say to thee? Should not thy heart break within
thee, at the contemplation of that infinite love
which would suffer thus for thee? Should not
thine eyes become a fountain of tears whenever
thou thinkest of such compassion? And should
not thy soul hate sin, henceforth, with perfect
hatred, and flee for refuge to the hope which the
immeasurable suffering of thy Savior sets before
thee?

" The pains of hell!" The horrors of abandonment! Under the pressure of this tremendous sorrow, lovingly encountered for man's redemption,
the heart of Jesus is literally broken, and His blood
is shed. Two brief and fervid utterances accom-
pany or follow this extreme suffering, and He
yields up the ghost.*

---

*When we speak of Jesus suffering the pains of hell, we do not
  necessarily mean that he endured every *variety* of suffering
  which the finally impenitent must endure. He could not

To hasten the death of the three who were crucified, "the soldiers came and brake the legs of the first, and of him that was crucified with him; but when they came to Jesus, and saw that He was dead already, they brake not His legs; but one of the soldiers pierced His side, and forthwith came there out   blood and water."* Physiologists tell us that this appearance of " blood and water," so distinct as to attract the attention of the faithful but unlearned disciple, indicates the previous separation of the vital fluid into its proximate elements, coagulum and serum. They tell us further, that such separation is not likely to occur *within* the blood vessels, but that it takes place rapidly when the blood has passed out of these into other cavities. The testimony of John thus indicates to us that physical death had resulted from the literal breaking of the heart, so that the blood was shed into the surrounding cavity. It was the consequence and effect of the penalty of sin, which Jesus, though without sin, took upon Himself for

have felt remorse for personal guilt, for he had no guilt. Yet as one person is sometimes brought into most intense sympathetic suffering for another, without knowing any reason for it, so Jesus may have suffered pangs identical with those of remorse and even those of despair ; and I doubt not that He did thus suffer.

*John 19. 34.

us; just as the physical death of the first Adam, though long delayed, was the direct consequence of the more awful spiritual death which he suffered for His own transgression.

It may be asked, 'If Jesus thus shed his own blood, or "laid down his own life," how can it be said that he was *slain?*' We have already seen that to be subject to temptation "like as we are," it was necessary that Jesus should come to earth and be "made in the likeness of men." He was thus able to partake of bodily and mental suffering such as human beings undergo. He was to view death from a human standpoint. He was to suffer as a criminal executed for transgression. His condemnation proceeded from the highest human tribunal in existence. He was deserted by the best of earth—by God's chosen people—by the very disciples who had so recently been ready to crown Him as their king. The step was now an easy and natural one, humanly speaking, to a sense of desertion by God the Father. It was the fitting moment for Satan's most cruel temptations. It was the fitting moment for the veiling of the Father's presence from the suffering Son. Outward cruelties were the occasion, not the cause, of that awful abandonment, the death which Jesus tasted for every man.

To illustrate this point, suppose a person standing upon the edge of a precipice, with a firm rock beneath his feet. Someone, with murderous intent, suddenly loosens that rock from its place, and the man falls headlong and is dashed to pieces. Strictly speaking, the cause of his death is concussion, and the cause of the concussion is gravitation. The loosening of the rock was the occasion of his death, not the cause; but it was the occasion without which the cause would not have been operative in producing death. The malicious act which *occasioned* death, was murder in the intention. But it was more ; it was murder in the act. No one could doubt this, nor that the dead man was murdered or slain.

So in the case before us. It seems from the sacred record that the immediate cause of the Savior's physical death was the bursting of the heart ; that the cause of this was the agony of soul death, or abandonment by the Father. The cause of this abandonment was the purpose of the Father and the Son, that the human race should be thus redeemed. But the occasion of this two-fold death was furnished by the malice of wicked, though highly professing men. This occasion was necessary to His death. " This which is written must yet be accomplished in me, And He was numbered with the transgressors.* Observe how often the word *must* occurs in the New Testament references to Christ's cruel treatment.†

The perfections of God necessitate the punishment of the sinner by separation from God—spiritual death. The perfections of God determine the primary means of rescue as redemption by substitution. The perfections of God and the lost state of man in the fall, necessitate the descent of the Son of God to earth, that He Himself may suffer the " chastisement of our peace." The lost, darkened state of the human race necessitates that the manifestation of the Divine perfections which Jesus gave in His teachings, His life and His sufferings, be made in the very presence of the utmost manifestations of human and Satanic malignity. And the Divine perfections necessitate that very malignity, in utmost and awful manifestation,as the one *essential occasion* by which the Holy One and the Just, even under the assumed limitations of the incarnation, could suffer for the unjust the penalty of spiritual death, the price of human redemption, and physical death as a consequence of the more awful suffering which chiefly constituted the atonement for sin.

---

*Lu. 22. 37. †Mat. 26. 54; Mk. 8. 31; Lu. 9. 22; 17. 25; 24.7, etc.

Peter therefore says correctly, " Him, being delivered by the determinate counsel and foreknowledge of God, ye have taken, and by wicked hands have crucified and *slain*."* " *Wicked hands*." "It must needs be that offences come, but woe to that man by whom the offence cometh."† Divine love and human malignity each has its part in " the great transaction ;" but the one loses nothing of its ineffable purity, and the other nothing of its awful guilt, by the fact that " thus it must be."

*Acts 2. 23.   †Mat. 18. 7.

CHAPTER XVI.

THE OFFERING OF CHRIST SUFFICIENT.

"It is finished." "Father, into thy hands I commend my spirit."—John 19. 30; Lu. 23. 46.

"IT is finished." A moment more and the lips of Jesus will be silent in death. But the brief interval between the extremity of suffering and the extinction of physical energy, is a moment of exultant joy. The great agony is over. God has "loosed the pains of death, because it was not possible that *He* should be holden of it."* This was first true in a spiritual, afterwards in a physical sense, the very order which prevails in the salvation of men. The atonement completed, the Savior is again in the bosom of the Father. There is no dread of the tomb. The great purpose of His descent to earth is accomplished, for even now He has tasted death for every man.† The inexorable yet reasonable demand of Divine justice is fully met, the price is paid, the human race redeemed. Some prophecies are yet to be fulfilled. That body, life-

---

*Acts 2. 24.

†In proof of this we have the positive statement of Peter, that " He bore our sins in His own body on the tree ;" not when His body was in the tomb, nor when in the garden, nor when the soul was separate from the body.

less ere long by the most positive evidence, must be laid in the tomb and be raised the third day. He must show " Himself alive after His passion by many infallible proofs,"* not merely to fulfill prophecy, but to assure His followers in all ages that " He ever liveth to make intercession for them,"† " that what he hath promised He is able also to perform ;"‡ that the offering of Himself will be *efficient* to every sinner who will accept it as his hope, unto the end of time. But the loud, triumphant " It is finished," is His own eternal attestation that the suffering He had just endured in His hour of darkness, is *sufficient* in the eyes of the *Father*. He could now say, with exultant joy, " Father, into thy hands I commend my spirit." If His expression of agony stands for inconceivable depths of anguish, His final exclamation denotes unmingled bliss. Henceforth He is the Savior of men ! Henceforth he that believeth in Him shall not perish, but have everlasting life ! He has vindicated God's justice by suffering for us its full measure in His own innocent person ; henceforth His name is above every name.

But how shall this offering be a propitiation for the whole world ? A simple mathematical illustra-

---

*Acts 1. 3.   †Heb. 7. 25.   ‡Rom. 4. 21.

tion has helped some, and may help others, as a stepping-stone to a higher, wider conception of the subject; though doubtless every illustration must fall short of an adequate expression of the great reality. Let us for a moment look at the question thus: Suppose a human being with an average capacity for joy or suffering, enduring for a single hour the Divinely appointed penalty for sin. Take that hour's suffering as the unit of a computation. Multiply this by the whole number of the human race, and the product is the sum of all penal suffering possible to the race, provided such suffering were limited to an hour's duration. But make it eternal. You must now multiply the product before obtained by the number of hours in eternity. This last factor is *infinite*. The product, therefore, which would stand for the sum of all penal suffering possible to the human family, is infinite.

Now mark the comparison. Suppose the suffering of the Son of God, when His soul was made an offering for sin, to have been only that of a sinful man with an average capability of joy or suffering, and suppose that suffering to have continued for an hour. It then corresponds exactly with the unit in our former computation, and falls infinitely short of meeting the demands of Divine justice.

It must have continued eternally, to be the redemption price of a single soul—the soul of Jesus must have been *left* in hell. But the expiatory suffering of Christ, was of short duration. Whence, then, its infinite value? What factor in it can make it an equivalent for the endless suffering of a condemned race? We find the answer in *the nature and character of Him who suffered*. Reflect a moment. The capability of joy from the Divine presence, or of suffering through separation from God, must be least in him who has least knowledge of God, least sense of His perfections and His love, and least in himself that corresponds with these. The posterity of Adam, apart from any Divine provision for their enlightenment, would therefore have had but a small capability of suffering, such as we are considering. Hell, in the sense of " destruction from the presence of God and from the glory of His power," could not be a bed of roses, even to these. It would be a state of unbridled passion, of endless discord and dissension, of sad unrest, of "everlasting burnings." But how much greater must be the pain of such a state to the soul which had caught some glimpses of the love of God and the peace of heaven, some sweet Divine instruction and some hope. How much keener still must be the sorrows of abandonment in the soul which had forsaken sin, answered love with love, and learned to delight in communion with the Holy One.   When, therefore, *the only-begotten Son of God* forsakes the infinite delights of the Father's presence and favor, and descends, though sinless still, to the companionship of *demons*, forsaken by Him for whom He had never felt an emotion at variance with perfect love —consider His infinite knowledge and His infinite love, His infinite holiness, and His infinite repugnance for sin—one does not hesitate to affirm that as the Savior's knowledge, love, holiness and dignity infinitely transcend those of the holiest man, so must the agony of His suffering have infinitely transcended that of which the best mere human being is capable.   In estimating the value of His sufferings for us, we have, therefore, an infinite factor and an infinite product; and as we seek to appropriate the wonderful benefits of the atonement, we exclaim with profoundest admiration and gratitude, and with peculiar emphasis, " He *is* the propitiation for our sins, and not for ours only, but also *for the whole world*."*

To this idea of equivalence some have objected, chiefly on the ground that if Christ thus bore the

*I. John 2. 2.

entire penalty for the sins of the race, Justice could not again inflict that penalty upon the race, nor upon any member of it, however sinful. Some have attempted to answer this objection by assuming that God the Father, in His foreknowledge of who would and who would not be saved, so *limited* the suffering of His Son as to make it an equivalent for the sins of those only who would accept salvation.

Both the objection and the above answer seem plausible, but both are shortsighted and mistaken. The plenitude of Christ's suffering for our redemption depends not upon its duration nor upon any other finite factor, but upon the one infinite factor— the excellence, dignity and capability of the Sufferer.* This same factor would have been present if He had suffered "the pains of hell" for but one

---

*In further illustration of this truth, it is sometimes said that a physical injury inflicted upon a human being, produces incomparably greater suffering than a like injury inflicted upon a beast ; because in man the body is joined with a rational soul. This must certainly be true, if mental suffering be considered ; for the human being considers the motive of the infliction, and the consequences to all concerned. Still the suffering is finite in value, because its subject is finite. In Jesus' suffering, there was the pain of a sinless, and therefore exquisitely sensitive body; there was the intense sorrow of a sinless and incomparably intelligent, rational soul; and there was likewise the participation of Deity Himself in all this anguish. Hence an infinite value, certainly.

individual, or suffered them but a moment. In other words, Christ, the Creator and Upholder of all things, could not have become an offering for sin at all, without His sacrifice being infinite and ample. *To taste death was the least that could have sufficed on His part for a single soul; it was all that was needed to make of* HIM *a sufficient sacrifice for all.*

But, while it is thus clear that the blessed atonement is ample even as a full mathematical equivalent, we are under no necessity of insisting upon such an equivalence. A perfect judicial satisfaction could be determined by the Judge alone. By Him mathematical equivalence might not be required. It is enough that His justice is fully satisfied and fully vindicated; and in Jesus both these objects are perfectly accomplished.

Whatever help we may have derived from the foregoing arithmetical comparison, are not our reverent hearts now prepared to leave this behind us, and in the fullness of living faith, and the fervor of holy devotion, to affirm our confidence that the plenitude of redemption rests in the plenitude of Christ Himself, and in the sublime fact that "God so loved the world that He gave His only begotten Son, that whosoever believeth in Him should not perish, but should have eternal life." All our just reasoning but brings us back to this simple truth, which in every age, to the learned and the unlearned, has been "the power of God unto salvation, through FAITH which is in Christ Jesus." How may our hearts rejoice, that long before our minds had clearly apprehended the wonderful nature of the Savior's work for us, we believed that Christ **died for the ungodly;" and a** faith toward God which we could not define nor explain, sprang **up** within us, and we were SAVED.

Again we stand in wonder before the wisdom, love and power of God, as manifested in Christ Jesus our Atonement; and before the infinite tenderness which makes faith alone in that finished work the ground on which the repentant, seeking soul may find life, and peace, and assurance forever.

To whom this plenteous provision shall be made *efficient*, and *on what conditions*, it is certainly the right of Him who has voluntarily prepared it, **to** determine.

CHAPTER XVII.

AN OPEN WAY.

"In whom we have redemption through His blood, the forgiveness of sins."—Eph. 1. 7.

THE great redemption is now an historic fact. "Those things which God had shown by the mouth of all His prophets that Christ should suffer, He hath so fulfilled."* SON OF MAN—for by that name, O Infinite Savior, thou art forever distinguished in the counsels of Heaven from the Father and the Holy Ghost, from angels and archangels—before thou wast lifted up thou saidst, "This is your hour and the power of darkness." Yet was the hour of deepest darkness peculiarly thine own; for it marked thee the Redeemer of men.† Thy humiliation was thy glory. Thenceforward do the saints on earth join with the prophets who were before them, in attributing their salvation to "the precious blood of Christ;"‡ and the saints in heaven, as they stand in thy glorified presence, exclaim in humble, reverent, grateful joy, "Thou art worthy * * for thou wast slain, and hast redeemed us unto God by thy blood."§

But why speak of salvation by the *blood?*   I—

*Acts 3. 18.   †John 17. 1.   ‡1 Pet. 1. 18, 19.   §Rev. 5. 9.

Because the shedding of Jesus' blood marks the completion of the agony which atoned for sin ; or in other words, marks the completion of the atonement, according to His own word. Not until this took place, or was taking place, did He cry, " It is finished." 2—Since it marks the depths of the Savior's suffering, it also indicates forcibly the Divine abhorrence of sin,* and the depth of the Divine love for the sinner.† 3—Because this word (blood), more perfectly than any other, associates the sacrificial death of Christ with those offerings which had been its significant type in every preceding age. 4—It means, in short, His giving His life a ransom for us. 5—Because His Blood is the token or sign which He presents before the Father as our plea.‡ 6—It is, by common consent of Christians, the memorial word of the great transaction which is the hope of the world. 7—For these reasons, this word, better than any other, expresses an intelligent faith in the fundamental and distinguishing doctrine of the Christian Scriptures, *salvation by redemption, redemption by substitution, and that the substitution of the Just for the unjust, the Infinite for the finite.*§

---

*See Heb. 12. 4.   †Rom. 8. 32, and Jno. 15. 13.   ‡See Lev. 16. 27; Heb. 9. 12.   § Those who through ignorance or false

The apostle having set forth his knowledge of and faith in the atonement, by saying, " We have redemption through His blood," then indicates a leading benefit of the atonement, " the forgiveness of sins." This does not mean, as some have vainly imagined, an unconditional and final forgiveness of the race, so that the death penalty for sin could not be inflicted upon the transgressor. As we have before seen, the offering was quite sufficient for this, if such an application of it had been consistent with its purpose, the salvation of men. But it must ever be borne in mind that the great offering was gratuitous, God having been under no obligation to provide it ; and that, therefore, He has an unquestionable right to determine the manner in which, the extent to which, and the conditions upon which its benefits shall accrue to the race or to the indivual. " Is it not lawful for me to do what I will with mine own ?" What His will *is* upon this subject, He has not left us to determine by our own

refinement shrink from the reverent use of this most expressive term, should acquaint themselves with the way of salvation, and learn by blessed experience to think and speak of "the precious blood of Christ" with the same reverent humility and grateful love as do "the just made perfect" in heaven. For some common errors on salvation by the blood of Christ, see App. K.

imperfect reasoning, but has very fully and clearly declared. We look, therefore, to His word to discover what the benefits of redemption are, and what limitations infinite Wisdom and Justice and Love has placed upon their application.

I. We thus learn that the first effect of the atonement is the removal of the legal barrier to salvation, *making the offer of salvation possible to a justly condemned race.** This is reconciliation in its judicial sense. It applies to every member of the human family, changing the relation of the entire race to the perfect law of God. Otherwise it could not be true in any sense that Jesus Christ " is the Savior of all men,"† or that whosoever will may take the water of life freely.‡ This reconciliation is unconditional, or without our co-operation; for " *when we were enemies,* we were reconciled to God by the death of His Son."§ It extends to every infant. It extends also to those who, having come to the years of understanding, have fallen under condemnation for their own transgression, securing to these the offer of salvation until they are saved, or until they have shown that they *will not* be saved.

This sublime effect of the atonement offering

---

*Rom. 3. 25, 26.   †I Tim. 4. 10.   ‡Rev. 22. 17.   §Rom. 5. 10.

opens the way for all its other effects, and is a sufficient guaranty of all else that is needful on God's part for human salvation ;* yet it would prove unavailing if not followed by another beneficent provision which must come from God only, and which nothing but the great atonement could procure.

II. The removal of the judicial barrier made the offer of salvation possible, not the salvation itself. For the state in which, but for the atonement, all of Adam's posterity must have been, was a state of utter darkness. The offer of salvation to persons in such a state, would be wholly unintelligible. No idea is fully developed except in presence of its opposite. The most vivid description of color or of the pleasures of sight, could impart no adequate idea of either to one who was blind from his birth. So the offer of light, life, peace, to those who were by natural law in a state of death, darkness and condemnation, must have been devoid of meaning. It could result in no adequate conception, desire or volition. A capacity for salvation must therefore be created. Our Savior meets this stubborn difficulty by actually lifting the race penalty in so far as to enable every child to receive and feel the direct influences of the Holy Spirit, to apprehend

*Rom. 8. 32.

the ideas of sin and righteousness, peace and condemnation. He confers, in short, a measure of spiritual life. "In Him was life, and the life was the light of men."* The measure of life so imparted is by Christ, and enables the soul to perceive or receive Christ. It will be forfeited by the child upon his first deliberate and willful transgression. Still it is life in such measure as to make salvation possible; life to the extent which may be necessary to make each person accountable for his own conduct and its results; and to make death as truly a direct personal penalty in the case of every transgressor as it was in the case of Adam.† But it is all of life that God could confer without us, and give us any part in our own salvation. Though it will not be retained unconditionally, it is conferred unconditionally, as necessary to render the other benefits of the atonement effectual. It is conferred upon every child. Otherwise it could not be said that Christ "lighteth every man that cometh into the world."‡ It is justification in so far as this could be conferred without the co-operation of our

---

*John I. 4. As "the light of the body is the eye," so the imparted life is the light of men. But as the eye cannot light the body unless it receives light from some luminous object, so the imparted life requires Divine illumination. See next paragraph. †For Bible proofs on this subject see Chap. V. ‡Jno. I. 9.

wills.   It is reconciliation in a moral sense, as denoting a definite though unconscious change in our
moral relation to God, and in so far as such reconciliation can be effected without our co-operation.
It is sometimes called passive justification.   The
conferring of life upon every child is, then, the second great result of our Savior's suffering for us.

III.   The third is the bestowal of Light in the
sense of illumination ; for in this sense also is Christ
the Light of the world.   By Him the irresponsible
are not only made receptive, but are actually illuminated—" every man that cometh into the world."
They are blest with the comforting, inspiring influence of the Holy Spirit, and with the ministrations
of holy angels.*   This important benefit of the
atonement, and the one which immediately precedes
it, the conferring of spiritual life, explain to us why
childhood seems so beautiful, and why it merits
our tenderest care.†   They also explain why little
children are so very susceptible to religious impres-
sions, and so intelligent in religious matters upon
so little instruction.   And they explain why the
child has those clear ideas of sin and righteousness which live so helpfully in the rational soul
after the spiritual life has been lost by sin ; and

---

*Mat. 18. 10.   †See Appendix L, Christ and the Children.

why outward nature so clearly speaks to every soul of God. And they explain as from God, that inclination to worship, which is commonly attributed to nature.

We may here pause to consider the condition of those children who die in infancy, or before they become capable of clearly understanding Divine law. The Bible is of course not addressed to such, and it says little about them. Certain conclusions, however, evidently merit our confidence.

1—Since Christ is the propitiation for the world, infants, who are a part of " the world," share the first benefit of the atonement, the removal of the legal barrier to salvation.

2—Since Christ " lighteth every man that cometh into the world," infants, being included in this number, share the second and third benefits of the atonement; being made receptive by the impartation of spiritual life, and being also illuminated by the inshining of Christ the Light.

3—These leading benefits, accruing as they do to every child, according to Scripture testimony, we may confidently claim the salvation of every child who dies innocent of conscious transgression, upon the warrantable assumption, applicable at every stage of the work of grace in a soul, that the effect-

ual conferring of any of the several benefits of redemption, is a guaranty of the conferring of all the
rest *if not resisted.*

4—Jesus said of little children, " of such is the
kindom of heaven." If " it is not the will of your
Father, that one of these little ones should perish,"
(and this expression, though it includes all begin-
ners in Christian experience, must from its connection include little children,) certainly they cannot
perish without resisting His will. If they die,
therefore, before such resistance is possible, all that
is needful for their complete sanctification and perfection is fully assured to them by the will of the
Father, and through the sacrificial death of Christ
our Savior.

Nor does this imply a sanctification after death ;
for how clearly God may speak to the infant who
is to be taken from earth, we know not ; nor do we
know, in the case of sudden death, how rapidly
conviction, instruction, faith and the response to
faith, may transpire in a soul already prepared for
the deeper work of grace, complete sanctification
by the baptism with the Holy Ghost.

We may also notice in this place the question
which very naturally arises when considering how
perfectly the atonement covers the needs of those

who die in infancy: Whether children may not be so well instructed during infancy, and so perfectly respond to that instruction in uniform and unhesitating obedience as not to need the new birth, but only the baptism with the Holy Ghost, when they reach the age of accountability. Upon this question it would be both needless and irreverent to speculate, since it is settled in the most positive manner *as a question of fact*, *by Divine testimony*. "There is not a just man upon the earth that doeth good and sinneth not.* "No man that sinneth not."† "If we say we have not sinned, we make Him a liar, and His word is not in us."‡ "Except a man be born again, he can not see the kingdom of God."§ We must remember, however, that these comprehensive declarations do not include infants; for it is clear that infants are not under the law, and "when there is no law, sin is not imputed."|| How comforting is the knowledge that our Savior thus secures the salvation of so large a portion of the race. Whether it is His will that so many shall die in infancy, is a question to be settled by other considerations than those which claim our attention in this volume.

---

*Eccl. 7. 20. †I. Ki. 8. 46. ‡I. Jno. 1. 10. §Jno. 3. 3.
||Rom. 5. 13.

CHAPTER XVIII.

FORGIVENESS OF SINS.

"In whom we have redemption through His blood, the forgiveness of sins."—Eph. 1. 7.

WE have now to consider those who, having
reached a clear knowledge of some portion
of the law of God, transgress that law, and so merit
eternal death as did Adam. It is clear that the
offer of salvation is possible to these, through the
purchased "forbearance of God."* "I came," said
Jesus, " not to call the righteous but sinners to repentance."† This shows not only that the offer is
possible, but that it is actually extended. The
same is shown by all the numerous offers and invitations of the Gospel to the sinner.

But the life once imparted, is gone. The word
is fulfilled, "The soul that sinneth, it shall die."
God's word now is, "Incline your ear and come
unto me ; hear, and your soul shall live."‡ Innocence has been exchanged for guilt, peace for condemnation, light for darkness. The offer of pardon
is not pardon. To transgressors Jesus says (for to
such, especially, is the Gospel sent), "Ye must be
born again."§ "Except ye be converted and be-

*Rom. 3. 25.   †Mat. 9. 13.   ‡Is. 55. 3.   §Jno. 3. 7.

come as little children, ye shall not enter into the
kingdom of heaven."*   To such the disciples exclaim, " As though God did beseech you by us, we
pray you in Christ's stead, be ye reconciled to
God."†   "Repent and be converted, that your sins
may be blotted out."‡

But if the life once imparted is gone, is not
the capacity for salvation also gone? It is not.
For that life, so lost, has left a definite impress on
the rational soul.   There remain, as an indelible
imprint, the ideas of accountability, of sin and
righteousness, of peace and condemnation. "Those
peaceful hours I once enjoyed, how sweet their
memory still." This has been the sigh of many a
soul for the restful innocence of childhood. The
natural conscience has received enlightenment that
will not pass away. The soul, now dead through
trespasses, has intelligibly set before it "life and
good, and death and evil." It has within it a
rational and moral basis for those powerful appeals of the Holy Spirit which will now come only
upon the plane of rational life, but will draw and
impel the soul to seek spiritual life.

In this way God has written His law in every
heart.§   Yet He cannot commune with the trans-

*Mat. 18. 3. †II. Cor. 5. 20. ‡Acts 3. 19. §Rom. 2. 15.

gressor by the continuous influx of His own life and light and joy. " The natural man receiveth not the things of the Spirit of God."* He must be addressed through reason and conscience, and by means which reason and conscience may apprehend. This brings us to the fourth great benefit of the Atonement.

IV. The various means of rational instruction, and the work of the Holy Spirit in witnessing through these in the rational soul. 1—The first of these means is an outward Divine revelation. This began in Adam, God Himself at first taking the place of an outward instructor, and speaking to Adam after the fall, probably, in an audible voice. The way of salvation thus made plain to our first parents, was doubtless accepted by them and handed down by them in their instructions to their posterity.† Later came prophecy, in which " holy men of God spake as they were moved by the Holy Ghost ;"‡ the law, which was received "by the disposition of angels ;"§ the psalms which, in both symbol and prophecy, so clearly " spake beforehand of the sufferings of Christ and the glory that should follow ;"*† the apostolic record of His life, death

---

*I Cor. 2. 14. †See Appendix H, An Early Revelation. ‡II Pet. 1. 21. §Acts 7. 53. *†I Pet. 1. 11.

and resurrection; the remaining books of the Bible —the selection and limitation of the contents of this wonderful volume being no less remarkable than its character. A large part of the Bible cannot be *understood or appropriated* by unaided human reason; but much of it may be, and it is one of God's chief means of instruction to the sinner as well as to the saint.

2—The example and precept of those who have received salvation. Upon moral questions the example of many who have not received salvation, may be helpful; for many of these have lofty ideas of personal integrity, and exemplify it in their associations with others. They "show the work of the law written in their hearts." On this account, if there were not a regenerate person upon earth, mankind, in virtue of the work of Christ, before described, would not be without examples of benevolence, kindness, amiability, pity, honesty and many other virtues, including even a degree of reverence. These could by no means exist in that perfection which is rendered possible by repentance toward God and faith in the Lord Jesus Christ, but would be quite sufficient to give added distinctness to every man's ideas of sin and righteousness.*

*Many persons conclude that, because unregenerate men have

3—The circumstances of life, which we call its providences, are means of Divine warning or instruction to us. Even while God "suffered all nations to walk in their own ways, He left not Himself without witness, in that He did good, and gave us rain from heaven, and fruitful seasons, filling our hearts with food and gladness."* Life's bounty and its privations, its successes and failures, its comforts and sufferings are often the means chosen by God to turn the hearts of the unregenerate to Him.

4—So is the order and harmony of nature, speaking everywhere of design, of providence, and goodness, and inviting us to consider our relation to the great and loving Sovereign of the universe.

And so wisely does the Holy Spirit dispose and use all these means of enlightment and persuasion, that every soul is supplied with sufficient incentives

---

good traits of character, there is in every man, apart from redemption, a natural goodness, which only needs be fostered to secure salvation. This unscriptural and anti-Christian idea is a dangerous mistake, and often, no doubt, a fatal one. We can see by the above, what is the real source of all the apparent excellencies of unregenerate men. If they would follow all the light they have, as well as they follow part of it, they would come to Christ and be saved. They would then discover how very little of real goodness their former character had held, and that the possession of that goodness gave them no merit whatever before God. "What hast thou that thou didst not receive?"

*Acts 14. 16, 17.

to solemn reflection and to earnest effort for salvation. When any of these means is allowed to awaken in us the consideration of our needs, our obligations, and the love of God for us, the result is conviction for sin, and a longing for pardon and acceptance from God. When this has resulted in a willingness and purpose to forsake all sin and walk in humble obedience, the penitent may ask and receive the fifth great benefit of the Atonement.

V. "The forgiveness of sins." This, in its very nature, implies the restoration of the life forfeited by transgression (this is called regeneration), and the removal of all sinward tendency, in so far as this had resulted from our own transgressions. This is God's own work in the soul, in consideration of the work of Christ for us, and in response to genuine repentance, and faith in Christ as our propitiation. The sinner cannot grow into forgiveness, nor into life, nor into adoption. These must be Divinely bestowed. He cannot earn them by faithfulness of conduct. They are freely conferred by God, and upon His own terms.

A clear proof of the supernatural element in conversion, is the exuberant joy that attends our pardon. It is something more than peace of conscience; for it is not proportioned to the remorse which preceded it. It has not a merely rational basis, for it is not proportioned to the clearness of our religious conceptions. It rests in our newly created life, an impartation from God. It links us with the joys of heaven and the powers of the world to come. It brings us to the embrace of a Father, for we have received the adoption of sons; and what child does not know that in the embrace of unselfish parental affection there is a deep, inspiring, transforming joy, beyond the power of language to express, or of reason to understand.

Another proof is the sudden capacity for light. God's truth lay all around us, and some portions of it could be understood by our natural reason; but much that we longed to know was veiled from us. Now, in a moment, we are changed, and needed truth is as clear to us as the faces of our friends.

Another proof is our changed affections, a standing mystery, but for God's own explanation. Why the hatred of once loved sins? Why the love of God's worship, His people, His word? Why the peculiar delight in secret prayer, and in the victory over sin? Why have some pleasures in a moment lost their hold upon us; and why do we so easily resist temptations which once seemed irresistible?

It is because we are " born from above." " A new heart will I give you, and a new spirit will I put within you."* Divine grace has linked us to Christ as our invincible Captain. HE giveth us the victory, and " we know that we have passed from death unto life."†

And to all this richness of experience Christ is the door, by the shedding of His own precious blood for us, " that whosoever believeth on Him should not perish, but should have eternal life."‡

---

*Ez. 36. 26.　†I Jno. 3. 14.　‡Jno. 3. 16.

CHAPTER XIX.

SANCTIFIED AND KEPT.

"We are sanctified by the offering of the body of Jesus Christ, once for all."—Heb. 10. 10.

VI.   But blessed as are the joys of pardon and regeneration—fit theme for enduring praise— the work of redemption reaches far beyond this stage of experience.   If this is glorious, there remains that which is far more glorious.   Sooner or later the regenerate become aware that the new life given at conversion, is placed side by side with a "body of death;"* an impediment to growth and to service, a source of much evil suggestion and even of direct resistance to the will of God.   This discovery is often surprising, and always painful.   It should never be discouraging ; for it is God's way of revealing a great need, and his preparation for revealing the Redeemer in a more transcendent light to the soul.

There are faults in our nature which are not consequences of our own transgression ; sinward tendencies which come to us by inheritance from a fallen ancestry. They are at variance with holiness,

*Rom. 7. 24.

and must be wholly removed before we are made meet for the kingdom of God. "The old man" must be "put off,"* "the body of sin destroyed,"† "the flesh" "crucified."‡ As this body of sin was ours without our transgression, it is not removed by our pardon. Yet it must be removed; for "without holiness, no man shall see the Lord."§Even the infant who dies must experience this change to prepare it for the unveiled presence of the Father. The provision for this work of cleansing by the baptism with the Holy Ghost, is the *sixth* great benefit of the atonement. For those who are enjoying the priceless blessings of forgiveness, the Savior prays, "Father, sanctify them through thy truth," thus denoting the means; Paul speaks of being "sanctified by the Holy Ghost," denoting the agency; and again, "we are sanctified by the offering of the body of Jesus Christ once for all," thus showing the atonement to be the great procuring cause.

When the Christian has yielded himself "unto God as those that are alive from the dead;" has presented his "body a living sacrifice;"** has made an uttermost consecration of himself to God, that he might be filled with the Holy Ghost; and has

---

*Eph. 4. 22.　†Rom. 6. 6.　‡Gal. 5. 24.　§Heb. 12. 14.　**Rom. 12. 1.

believed in the finished redemption as the purchase
and guaranty of this wonderful gift of grace, he enters
the Sabbath rest prepared for the people of God.*
He receives in the gift of the Holy Spirit an earnest of his incorruptible inheritance.† He is filled
with the fulness of God.‡ There was at conversion
a receiving of the Holy Ghost, there was His presence as a guide, keeper, instructor, comforter; but
it is the *baptism* with the Holy Spirit, the being
filled with Him, which the Bible calls the *gift* of
the Holy Ghost. If the former experience (regeneration) was life, this is life more abundant—the
preparation of the soul for heaven, the preparation
for the most effectual service on earth.

As we behold this marvelous work of grace in
ourselves and others, we again look back upon our
suffering Christ, and exclaim with greater contri-
tion, greater humility, greater self-abasedness than
ever before, "Worthy is the Lamb that was slain,
to receive power, and riches, and wisdom, and
strength, and honor, and glory, and blessing."§ By
example and precept He has taught us to resist sin,
and how to resist it. But the power to follow that
example and that precept, to overcome the world,
to stand against the wiles of the devil, and to bring

*Heb. 4. 9.   †Eph. 1. 14.   ‡Eph. 3. 19.   §Rev. 5. 12.

forth fruit unto God, comes through sanctification of the Spirit, as truly the purchase of the Savior's blood as is the pardon of our transgressions.

In thus speaking and thinking of the work of sanctification, let it never be forgotten that the Holy Spirit is not a mere influence, but a Divine Person to whom belong the same attributes which characterize the Father and the Son. He it is who convinces the world of sin, of righteousness, and of judgment; who, as the representative of the Father, draws all men toward Christ; who works in the heart of the sinner godly sorrow and repentance, and who witnesses to our salvation when we have repented and believed in Jesus; who comforts, guides and keeps the trusting believer; who reveals to him his carnality, and makes him long for holiness. Yet He is *sent by the Father and the Son*, a gift to the believer who prepares his heart for this holy, heavenly occupant by a perfect surrender, dedication and faith. He is, with the Father and the Son, a proper object of worship and prayer, and of the most loving and grateful devotion.

VII. The happy relation into which the believer is brought by regeneration, is fraught with manifold other blessings. "If I would declare and speak of them, they are more than can be num-

bered." Prominent among them, and worthy of
especial mention, is the power to prevail with God
in prayer, in the name of the Son. This blessing
is most fully realized after the experience of complete sanctification has been received, though
enjoyed in large measure by many consecrated souls
who have not received that experience. "If ye
abide in me, and my words abide in you, ye shall
ask what ye will and it shall be done unto you."*
"And whatsoever ye shall ask in my name, that
will I do, that the Father may be glorified in the
Son. If ye ask anything in my name I will do
it."† Blessed Christ, how can thy saints sufficiently
adore thee? Thou dost not only conform them to
thine image, but dost lovingly unite them to thyself. They may pillow their heads upon thy bosom.
They may pour into thy loving heart their com-
plaints as well as their praises. They may approach
the infinite Father in thy sacred name, O infinite
Son. And dost thou indeed hear the crying of the
poor, and the sighing of the needy?‡ Does the cry
of the oppressed enter into thine ears? When my
father and my mother forsake me, will the Lord
take me up?§ To them that mourn in Zion wilt
thou give beauty for ashes, the oil of joy for mourn-

*John 15. 7.   †Jno. 14. 13, 14.   ‡Ps. 12. 5.   §Ps. 27. 10.

ing, the garment of praise for the spirit of heavi-
ness?* Wilt thou in temptations, trials, and
dangers, keep them as the apple of thine eye?†
Yes, dear Redeemer, thou hast said it. We could
not believe it but for thy word, nor receive it but
by thy blood ; and thou hast bowed thy heavens
and come down, and hast given us both. In thee
do we hope, our blessed Advocate and Intercessor.

VIII. Our Advocate ! This word suggests another benefit of the atonement, so singular that we
could not believe it but for the Divine word.
Though the regenerate are less likely to commit sin
than the unregenerate, and the wholly sanctified
less likely than the merely regenerate, yet both
classes of believers experience temptations and may
yield to them. It is well known that many believers backslide in conduct, and become very nearly
assimilated to the sinful, unbelieving world. This
indicates a previous unfaithfulness, a backsliding of
heart. Even those whose hearts are, in the main,
true as steel, who would not deliberately transgress
the known will of God, may be suddenly impelled
to actions, expressions or thoughts which are sinful, notwithstanding the possibility of being con-
tinuously preserved from this. Probably very few

*Is. 61. 3.   †Deut. 32. 10.

persons live any great length of time without some conscious transgression.

What, now, is the relation of the Christian to the Divine law after transgression? Jesus says, "Whosoever committeth sin, is the servant of sin."* John says, "He that committeth sin is of the devil."† From these and similar statements we might infer that the penalty of sin is at once visited upon every believer who sins, and that if such are restored, regeneration must be repeated. This, however, is not a necessary inference. Beyond all contradiction, perfect justification or sanctification cannot be known, so long as even the slightest sin rests upon the soul. Nor can perfect communion be enjoyed, nor perfect service rendered. The saint who sins, even in thought, increases the existing sinward tendency of his own heart; or if he were wholly sanctified, *creates* in his heart such a tendency, a body of sin. His soul is brought, in a measure, under bondage, and all the work of grace hitherto experienced is endangered. But as yet the death penalty is *suspended*. Opportunity is still given to attest the purpose of the heart by repentance and faith, more humble and perfect than ever; and to make our very sin a

*John 8. 34. †I John 3. 8.

means of future grace to us in an increased sense of our insufficiency, an increased knowledge of the deceitfulness of sin, an increased watchfulness and consecration to Him who giveth us the victory, an increased power to encourage the fallen.

In the matter of salvation, God so honors the work of His dear Son that when once we have turned with full purpose of heart to Him, and are overcome by some sudden or unknown temptation, His mercy waits, and His agencies conspire to bring us again not only into the former relation, but even into a more perfect enjoyment of that relation. We are, for Christ's sake, held in a state of reprieve until we thus return to God, or until we are hopelessly backslidden and will not be saved.

John clearly indicates this in writing to believers, "My little children, these things write I unto you, that ye sin not; and if any man sin, we have an advocate with the Father, Jesus Christ the righteous."* The same thought is present in the numerous reproofs and warnings to the churches.† The teaching of John is clear and positive: "If any man see his brother sin a sin which is not unto death, he shall ask, and He shall give him life for them that sin not unto death. There is a

*I John 2. 1. †I Cor. 3. 1-4; I Cor. 5. 6; Rev. 2. 3, etc.

sin unto death ; I do not say that he shall pray for
it. All unrighteousness is sin, and there is a sin
not unto death."* From this it is clear that even
"a brother" may sin a "sin unto death," but that
death is not awarded him until he has thus sinned.
This wonderful benefit of the atonement does not,
however, give the Christian the smallest license to
sin. He who would thus abuse it, thinking to be
saved at last by Divine mercy, insults that mercy,
tempts Omnipotence, and adds sin to sin. No
Christian can sin in the least without danger. His
only safety is in the obedience of faith. But deliberate sin is especially dangerous. No one who sins
knows the moment when his will may pass beyond
the possibility of effectual repentance, and consign
him to despair. "Watch and pray, that ye enter
not into temptation."† "I say unto all, Watch."‡

---

*I John 5. 16, 17.   †Mat. 26, 41.   ‡Mark 13. 37.

CHAPTER XX.

PERFECTED FOREVER.

"For by one offering He hath perfected forever, them that are sanctified."—Heb. 10. 14.

IX.   But the work of redemption is not complete at the baptism with the Holy Ghost, nor even at that establishment in grace from which we shall never fall.   Conformed in heart to the image of the Son, having Christ within, the hope of glory, the ripest saint on earth yet waits for the redemption of his body.*   His physical frame is not the perfect servant of the new, pure heart God has given him. His body is feeble.   Its motions and features yet speak of sinful action and thought, now done away, it is true, but yet marking the body as having been the servant of sin.   The body retains habitudes which, though no longer sinfully indulged, yet suggest sin.   If no longer a source, they are at least a means of temptation.   And so marked is the bodily nature in this way, that it is the channel through which even truly sanctified parents communicate sinful tendencies to their offspring. Moreover, these bodies are perishable.

*Rom. 8. 23.

And has the Atonement provided something better? It has. "This corruptible must put on incorruption, and this mortal must put on immortality."* "We look for our Savior the Lord Jesus Christ, who shall change our vile body, that it may be fashioned like unto His glorious body."† "The last enemy that shall be destroyed is death." How wonderful is the Divine order in salvation, conforming exactly to that of the fall. The steps in that melancholy event were unbelief, transgression, death, moral depravity, mental depravity, physical corruption and physical death. In the return the steps are faith, repentance, life, moral cleansing, mental cleansing, and resurrection. Every man suffers all that is contained in the first list. Every man may experience all that is contained in the second; for the great salvation embraces all. "We know," says the apostle, "that if our earthly house of this tabernacle were dissolved, we have a building of God, a house not made with hands, eternal in the heavens."§ The wicked also will have a resurrection, but it will be "to shame and everlasting contempt."*† Only they who cleansed by the blood of Christ, shall rise in His image. "These are they which came out of great

*I Cor. 15. 53.   †Phil. 3. 20, 21.   ‡I Cor. 15. 26.   §II Cor. 5. 1.
   *†Dan. 12. 2.

tribulation and have washed their robes and made them white in the blood of the Lamb. THERE-FORE are they before the throne of God."* We record, then, as the ninth great benefit of the Atonement, the resurrection of the saints in the image of Christ.

X. And then the coronation by Christ's own loving hand. " Henceforth there is laid up for me a crown of righteousness, which the Lord the righteous Judge shall give me at that day, and not to me only, but to all them also that love His appearing."† " If we suffer, we shall also reign with Him."‡ " Be thou faithful unto death, and I will give thee a crown of life."§ " To him that overcometh will I grant to sit with me in my throne, even as I also overcame and am set down with my Father in His throne."*† " And they shall reign forever and ever."*‡

---

*Rev. 7. 14, 15. †II Tim. 4. 8. ‡II Tim. 2. 12. §Rev. 2. 10.
*†Rev. 3. 21. *‡Rev. 22. 5.

CHAPTER XXI.

COMPLETE IN HIM.

"For it became Him for whom are all things and by whom are all things, in bringing many sons unto glory, to make the Captain of their salvation perfect through sufferings."

—Heb. 2. 10.

XI. We have now seen Jesus as the necessary and the sufficient sacrifice for sin. We have seen why, through Him, the offer of salvation is possible to all, and why it is made to all. We have seen also why the irresponsible are saved, and why an infinitely holy and unchanging God can pardon the sinner who repents and believes in Jesus. We have also seen that, according to the Holy Scriptures, numerous other benefits follow pardon in the case of those who continue to walk with God, the last of these benefits being exaltation to a crown and kingship eternal with Christ. But why all these benefits result from the death of Christ, has not been clearly shown. If that death was truly an atonement for sin, then the removal of the penal and other consequences of sin from those who, by the Divine decree, are eligible to the benefits of the atonement, must follow as a necessary and logical consequence of the atonement itself. But how should it follow that innumerable incentives are freely given to an offending race to come and receive the great salvation? How should it follow to the Christian that "ye shall ask what ye will and it shall be done unto you?"* Why should the Christian who sins be held in a state of reprieve and be able to seek pardon in the name of an Advocate? Finally, why should sinners saved by grace be not only saved to the estate of Adam before he fell, but be actually glorified with Christ?

To these questions the true and sufficient answer is to be found in the peculiar relation in which our Redeemer, *because of His atonement, and its recognition by the Father*, stands to mankind, and especially to the believer.

1—Primarily He is our Redeemer. "Ye are not your own; for ye are bought with a price."† As His purchased possession we are objects of His special care, and subject—so far as we permit ourselves to be—to His ever loving will.

2—He is our High Priest.‡ It was in this capacity that He offered up Himself as a sacrifice, and that He entered into heaven itself,§ by His own blood,** now to appear in the presence of God for

---

*John 15. 7. †I Cor. 6. 19, 20. ‡Heb. 4. 14. §Heb. 9. 24.
**Heb. 9. 12.

us. In this capacity also He instructs His people, gives power to every means of grace, and is the "one mediator between God and man."*

3—He is our Brother. "That He might be a merciful and faithful High Priest, it behoved Him to be made like unto His brethren."† In that He Himself hath suffered, being tempted, he is able to succor them that are tempted."‡ Hence we are objects of His everlasting compassion. Nothing is wanting which may be needful to secure our perfect restoration to the Father's favor. In this loving relation He becomes our tender Shepherd, entrusted with our feeding, our guidance and our protection. "The Lamb which is in the midst of the throne shall feed them, and shall lead them unto living fountains of waters."§

4—Jesus Christ is not only our Brother, but He is the First-born,** in the sense of having in all things the preeminence; *† the one competent and perfect representative of the redeemed race before God, as He is also the perfect representative of God to man. The burden of His loving heart must ever be to win as many as possible to the Father's favor, and to present them faultless before His throne.*‡

5—To His true followers He holds the relation

*I Ti. 2. 5. †Heb. 2. 17. ‡Heb. 2. 18. §Rev. 7. 17. **Rom. 8. 29. *†Col. 1. 18. *‡Rev. 14. 5 ; Jude 24.

of the Head to the other members of the body.* To such it is said, " It is God which worketh in you, both to will and to do of His good pleasure."† In virtue of this relation of Christ to the church, there is ever present with them a supernatural Divine power sufficient for every need. But there is also an unutterable sympathy and a jealous guardian-ship, so vividly represented in the expression, " He kept him as the apple of His eye."‡

6—Again, He is our Prince.§ His saints are His subjects. Their perfection must enhance His glory and His joy. It must enhance the Father's glory, which is ever the Son's delight.

7—Finally, He is our Captain—a Prince in ac-tion, at the head of His forces, leading those who trust in Him, to certain victory. " He teacheth my hands to war, and my fingers to fight."** But this captaincy is not a mere official relation to the redeemed. It is infinitely more than this. The love which prompted Him to become " the author of eternal salvation to all them that obey Him,"*† prompted Him to assume to these the tender, yet potent relation of their federal Head. As Adam, " who is the figure of Him that was to come,"*‡ was

---

*Eph. 4. 12–16. †Phil. 2. 13. ‡Deut. 32 10. §Acts 5. 31.
**Ps. 144. 1. *†Heb. 5. 9. *‡Rom. 5. 14.

the head of the human family, representing it in his condemnation, and imparting to it the bent of his own fallen nature, so Christ Jesus becomes the head of his followers,* representing them in separation, trial and victory, and imparting to them the same mind that was in Him. The Father views them in Him, accepts them in Him,† claims them and treats them as sons because of Him.‡ They also are to see *themselves* in Him, crucified with Him,§ dead to sin with Him,** alive in Him,*† victorious in Him,*‡ and the great concern of their life, for themselves, is to " *be found in Him.*"*§

Rest, assurance faith, hope, love, patience, long-suffering, humility, self-denial, utter consecration, courage, strength, zeal in service, victory, and unspeakable consolation and joy flow from the believer's proper recognition of the headship of Christ. Christ's offering is his offering; Christ's faith is his faith; Christ's conquest, his conquest; "And ye are complete in Him, who is the head of all principality and power; in whom also ye are circumcised with the circumcision made without hands, in putting off the body of the sins of the flesh by the circumcision of Christ; buried with

---

*Eph. 1. 22. †Eph. 1, 6. ‡Gal. 4. 4–7. §Gal. 2. 20. **Rom. 6. 10, 11. *†Rom. 6. 10, 11. *‡I Cor. 15. 57. *§Phil. 3. 8, 9.

Him in baptism, wherein also ye are risen with Him, through the faith of the operation of God, who hath raised Him from the dead. And you, being dead in your sins, and the uncircumcision of your flesh, hath He quickened together with Him, having forgiven you all trespasses, blotting out the handwriting of ordinances that was against us, which was contrary to us, and took it out of the way, nailing it to His cross."* "Our old man is crucified with Him, that the body of sin might be destroyed, that henceforth we should not serve sin."† "God forbid that I should glory, save in the cross of our Lord Jesus Christ, by whom the world is crucified unto me, and I unto the world."‡ "We are more than conquerors, through Him that loved us."§ *In Him* the dominion of sin is forever broken. The awakened sinner finds he cannot do the things that he would.** The believer finds "I can do all things through Christ which strengtheneth me."*†

But it is the high privilege of the true believer not only to see himself thus in Christ, but also to see God in Christ,*‡ and thus the blessed union of himself with God. "As thou Father art in me, and

---

*Col. 2. 10–14. †Rom. 6. 6. ‡Gal. 6. 14. §Rom. 8. 37. **Gal. 5. 17. *†Phil. 4. 13. *‡II Cor. 5. 19.

I in thee, that they also may be one in us."*
Amazing grace! Infinite tenderness! Truly "help
is laid on One that is mighty."†

It is because of the headship of Christ over all
who accept Him and abide in Him, that he speaks
of them as His bride, and of Himself as husband,
thus using that which He intended as the purest,
tenderest, sweetest earthly relationship, to depict to
us in a single figure His infinite love and minute
and watchful care over those who are His.

It is because of the wonderful relationship of
Jesus to His church, that the believer is able to ask
the Father in Jesus' name. It is likewise because
of this relationship that the truly converted are
heirs of all things, having, *by covenant*, all that is
necessary for their perfection, their service, their
everlasting peace. To have all these *by possession*,
they have only to *abide in Him, and exercise appro-
priating faith in the moment of need*. Such faith
is of course always conditioned on perfect self-
surrender , an ever new and complete abandonment
to Him.

And it is this headship of our risen Lord, which
is the guaranty of the ultimate perfection of all
true believers. When any of these are prevented,

---

*Jno. 17. 21.   †Ps. 89. 19.

without their own fault, from fully knowing or following the will of God, or when any of them die in the early stages of Christian growth, their entire sanctification and perfection is fully assured by the headship of Christ.

One cannot ponder intelligently the wonderful relations in which the Savior stands to those whom the Father hath given Him, without discerning in these relations and in the oneness of the Savior with the Father, the sufficient reason why the saints are so perfectly supplied with every means of grace while here, and glorified with Christ in the world beyond; and why such powerful incentives are offered to sinners to come unto Him.

Yet these relations are inseparably connected with His vicarious death for us. As the Son of God, He was perfect before the world was made; but as High Priest, Elder Brother, Shepherd, Head, Prince, Captain, He was made "perfect through sufferings;"* becoming all of these in the truest, fullest sense through that suffering by which he became our Redeemer. Observe how forcibly this thought is expressed by the apostle to the Gentiles: "Who (Christ Jesus) being in the form of God, thought it not robbery to be equal with God,

*Heb. 2. 10.

but made Himself of no reputation, and took upon Him the form of a servant, and was made in the likeness of men; and being found in fashion as a man, He humbled Himself and became obedient unto death, even the death of the cross. Wherefore God hath highly exalted Him, and given Him a name which is above every name; that at the name of Jesus, every knee should bow, of things in heaven, and things on earth, and things under the earth; and that every tongue should confess that Jesus Christ is Lord, to the glory of God the Father."* We may reckon, therefore, as another glorious benefit of Christ's death for sinners, His exaltation by God the Father to that intimate and varied relation to the redeemed, which makes their perfection and exaltation His care and His delight; while at the same time all power is given unto Him in heaven and in earth; so that none that trust in Him shall perish, nor shall any be able to pluck them out of His hand.

Thus, logically and naturally, are assured to believers in Jesus those amazing benefits of the Atonement which are clearly asserted in the Scriptures, but which may not appear to follow as direct and necessary consequences of His vicarious suffering.

---

*Phil. 2. 6–11.

CHAPTER XXII.

WHAT MANNER OF LOVE.

"For God so loved the world."—John 3. 16.

XII. An inestimable benefit of the great Atonement is its constraining and restraining power upon the human mind, as a *revelation of the love of God*. It lays open to us the Father's heart, with its tenderness, and pity, and well-wishing, with its spirit of self-sacrifice for our salvation. In His unutterable suffering for us, the Lord Jesus exhibits to us the mind of the Father. There is nowhere the slightest compromise with sin, nor a question as to its just deserts, nor a disposition to save men in their transgressions. On the contrary, there is an unyielding repugnance to sin, a most reverent regard for the Divine law, a consummate vindication of the judgment of God against all unrighteousness. But this testimony of Jesus involves the sacrifice of Himself. We have endeavored to look, by the help of the Sacred Record, upon that depth of anguish which evoked the cry, "My God, my God, why hast thou forsaken me?" Certainly we cannot forget that the only conceivable motive in the mind of the Son or the Father was infinite, incomprehensible LOVE. Nor can we cease to thank and praise Him for this incontestible *proof* of love. To the vilest sinner, the messenger of the gospel, fresh from the contemplation of Christ's sufferings, can say, " *God loves you.*" Many a sin-burdened soul has been arrested by this strange, yet blessed announcement, and despair has given place to hope ; and then, as proof was furnished in the story of the *cross*, that weary soul has *believed* and been *saved from sin.*

The memory of the cross as a proof of Divine love, is one of the mightiest preventives of back-sliding. If God considered thy salvation worth so much ; if He could give His only begotten Son ; if that Son, moved by the same impulse, could thus suffer and die for thee, how dreadful to sin against a love like that ! And how dreadful sin must be, to call forth such a manifestation of love ! Redeemed soul, how canst thou, *in sight of Calvary*, consent to a moment's indulgence of the most promising temptation ? How sadly must love be wronged, Infinite Love, which could forego years of heavenly pleasure and suffer exquisite pangs for thy sake, if thou canst not for His sake deny thyself the pleasures of sin forever !

But the love of God as manifested in Christ is

also a potent incentive to positive holiness. Love like that will not fail thee, Christian, in thine hour of trial, nor suffer thee to be put to confusion. It is a sufficient ground for thy faith and hope in every conflict. This is not all. The cross of Christ pleads with thee more eloquently than words could do, challenging *thy* love. More plainly than in words does it say, " My son, *give me thy heart*." It constrains thee to abandon thyself to Him, to be His, and only His, forever. It constrains thee to follow where he leads, to be filled with His Spirit, to spend and be spent for the glory of God and the salvation of men. It enables thee to " count all things loss for the excellency of the knowledge of Christ Jesus [thy] Lord." It enables thee to endure hardness; to encounter perils; to labor obediently, devotedly, where there is no apparent fruit; to love and labor where thou art not loved. It teaches thee, and it helps thee, to manifest thy own love in self-sacrifice; to be willing to suffer shame, persecution, ostracism, the spoiling of thy goods, bodily pain, and even death for Him, *that some might be saved*. This is the true spirit of cross-bearing. How many, it may be asked, of those who profess salvation by the Lord Jesus Christ, really know what it is to take up their cross daily and follow Him? Yet without this they are not His disciples. Let them *consider Him*, who endured the cross, despising the shame, and their hearts must grow more humble, more penitent, more fervent, more rich in all the fruits of the Spirit. And let them not forget that He *liveth*, to make intercession for them ; to secure the fulfillment of His precious promises to them ; to baptize them with the Holy Ghost, "that Christ may dwell in [their] hearts by faith ; that [they] being rooted and grounded in LOVE, may be able to comprehend, with all saints, what is the breadth, and length, and depth, and height ; and to know the love of God, which passeth knowledge, that [they] might be filled with all the fullness of God."

To every human heart that is open to receive it, the suffering of our Lord as revealing the love of God toward us, is the most powerful influence for correction, for consolation. for assurance, for con-straint to holiness and to service. Love, Love, in-finite, self-sacrificing Love ! Sinner, couldst thou contemplate it for a moment, methinks thy heart must cry out, " Draw me, I will run after thee ;" and then thou wouldst become aware of the great burden upon thy back, the guilt of committed sin, the certainty of its awful deserts ; and thou wouldst be enabled to see thy loving Lord bearing these deserts *for thee* that thou through repentance and faith mightest be saved. And then, as thy heart confided in Him as thy Savior and Redeemer, seeking pardon and a new heart through Him only, thou wouldst find thy burden gone; thy heart transformed, reconciled; thy soul sustained and filled with heavenly love; and thy tongue could say in rapture, "*I know* that my Redeemer liveth."

Thus the great Atonement stands before us, a transaction simple in its nature yet manifold in its relations and results, revealing in one view the corruption and malignity of the human heart, and the holiness and love of God; the just and awful penalty of sin, and the unspeakable joys of salvation; the helplessness of man without Christ, and his sublime possibilities in Christ.

In the light which Holy Scripture throws upon this great transaction, one intelligent look at the Crucified One has in it more illuminating, transforming power than a life-time study of human philosophies; one moment of child-like faith in the suffering, dying, risen Savior, than a lifetime of the severest morality. For that look and this faith are the open door through which Divine power hastens to enter, that it may begin, unfold and perfect the astounding miracle of a new creation in the image of God.* "What the law could not do, in that it was weak though the flesh, God, sending His own Son in the likeness of sinful flesh and for sin, condemned sin in the flesh, that the righteousness of the law might be fulfilled in us who walk not after the flesh but after the Spirit."† "Thanks be unto God who giveth us the victory, through our Lord, Jesus Christ!"

Let us now recount the several most striking benefits of the Savior's death, fully assured to all who receive Him, by His present, eternal life.

I. The removal of the legal barrier to salvation, so that God might be unchangeably just, and yet justify the sinner who believes in Jesus.

II. The creation of a capacity for salvation, by the impartation of life to every child; this life being the light of men, as the eye is the light of the body.

III. The illumination of every man that cometh into the world.

IV. The various means of rational instruction through which the Holy Spirit speaks, even to those who have become dead through trespasses.

---

*Col. 3. 10.   †Rom. 8. 3, 4.

V.   Pardon for the sinner who repents and believes in the Lord Jesus Christ as his Savior.

VI.   The complete sanctification of the believer by the baptism with the Holy Ghost.

VII.   The power to prevail in prayer in Jesus' name.

VIII.   Reprieve or suspension of penalty to the Christian who sins "a sin not unto death."

IX.   Resurrection in the image of Christ.

X.   A throne with Him in His kingdom.

XI.   The exaltation of Jesus Christ to that supreme relation to the redeemed, which is a perfect guaranty to every irresponsible person and to every true believer, of all the above-named benefits of the atonement.

XII.   And finally, that incomparable revelation of Divine love to men, which appeals irresistibly to every true heart as an incentive to forsake all and follow Him.

Blessed Redeemer, do all these wonderful provisions for salvation belong to the riches of thy grace ?   Are they the purchase of thy blood ?   They are. Not one of them could ever accrue to us without thy death. By that death they are all made ours if we but will. I thank thee that *thou hast died for me.* I admire the inspiring example of thy spotless, holy life; I dwell in mute wonder upon thy inimitable precepts; I delight to contemplate thy marvelous humiliation and thy ascended glory. Each of these has its inestimable part in thy work for my salvation. But not all of these, my risen Lord, so kindle my heart with the fervor of holy devotion as does the memory of thy suffering. Thou art indeed my Counsellor and my Exemplar, my High Priest, my Elder Brother, my Prince, my Captain; but thou art also, and first, my SACRIFICE.

> "Nothing in my hand I bring;
> Simply to thy cross I cling;"

for thou hast borne for me my griefs and carried for me my sorrows. Infinite is thy love. Thou art God over all, blessed forever; yet art thou also "the Lamb of God, which taketh away the sin of the world." Through all the years of my accountability, thy blood has pleaded for me before the mercy seat. In my infancy it covered me. In my manhood it cleansed me, Oh, how wondrously! Through thy blood accepted as my plea, thou hast become my Leader, Comforter, Defender, my all in all. Through this do I humbly cry, "Abba, Father." Through this do I receive the sanctifying fulness of the Holy Ghost. And if at thy coming

I shall be worthy to stand in thy unveiled presence and behold thy glory, and shall be by thee presented faultless before the Father, it will be because THOU ART WORTHY, AND WAST SLAIN, AND HAST REDEEMED ME UNTO GOD BY THY BLOOD. Amen.

APPENDICES.

APPENDICES.

APPENDIX A.

THE DOCTRINE OF FUTURE PUNISHMENT.

WHETHER hell is, and what it is, are not questions of speculation, but of fact. There are just two ways of directly determining such questions. One is by experience, the other by testimony. In the case before us, experience fails. None of us can, while living upon this earth, be in precisely the state of the finally impenitent after final judgment. For even the worst sinner upon earth derives some encouragement from false hopes, and some comfort from diversions, and from the Divine influences which prevail in the world about him. Our knowledge of the state of lost souls must therefore rest upon testimony. But, for the reasons already given, it cannot rest upon human testimony. Have we any other ? Most certainly, the word of our Savior. In Him " are hid all the treasures of wisdom and knowledge."* " And we know that His testimony is true."† His word upon any point is therefore final. He *knows* and He is *true*.

---

*Col. 2. 3. †John 1, 17.

What, then, has this witness said upon the state of the finally impenitent?

1—He calls it *hell*. Mat. 5. 22, 29; 10. 28; 18. 9; 23. 33, etc.

2—He describes it as a state of *torment*. Mat. 8. 29; 25. 41, 46; Mk. 9. 43, 44; Lu. 13. 28; 16. 24, 28.

3—He represents the state as *endless*. Mat. 25. 41, 46; Mark 3. 29; Lu. 16. 26; Mat. 12. 32; Mark 9. 43-48.

4—His testimony leaves no doubt at all that some will receive this punishment. This is suffici-ently shown by the above references.

It may be asked, Did not Jesus, when speaking of this subject, use metaphoric language? At times He may have done so, but not more than when speaking of heaven. If the description fails in one case because figurative language is employed, would it not fail in the other case for the same reason? If hell is not to be dreaded and shunned as a reality, is heaven to be hoped for and sought as a reality? Certainly no reasonable person can doubt that the language of Christ respect-ing heaven and hell, denotes important and widely contrasted *realities*. And when He speaks of each as "*eternal*," it seems difficult not to understand that both are *enduring* realities.

Those who disbelieve the doctrine of future punishment, or of eternal punishment, affirm that the Old Testament word *Sheol* and the New Testament word *Hades*, the former of which, in the Authorized Version is sometimes translated "hell," and as often "the grave;" and the latter of which is, except in one instance, always translated "hell," really meant only the grave, or at most the unseen world. To my own mind this affirmation is without proof. One can hardly examine the passages in which these words occur, and compare them with other Scripture bearing upon the subject, without concluding that "Hades" always, and "Sheol" generally, meant something *more* than the grave. In thirty-one places "Sheol" is translated *the grave*; but in only a few, if any, of those places is it clear that a mere burial place is intended. In thirty-one places the same word is translated *hell*; in most of these places it is clear that something *more* than a burial-place is meant. It is a remarkable fact that where the gave is mentioned in our Authorized Version in connection with a possessive, as, "Rachel's grave," "Abner's grave," "his grave," "my grave," "your graves," and when the thought is pleasant, peaceful, respectful, or tender, the word used is *never* "Sheol." On the

contrary, where sorrow, shame and punisment
are connected with it, the word is *always*
"Sheol." It is also true that where the translators
have rendered "Sheol" as *hell*, the term is associ-
ated with sorrow, pain, sin, condemnation, and
personal suffering. So that the word in these
places clearly denotes, not the burial place of
the dead, but the *state* of the dead, and particularly of the *wicked* dead. It is difficult to see how
any candid investigator of the Old Testament could
doubt for a moment that the punishment of the
wicked by conscious suffering after death is certainly and repeatedly taught in that great reposi-
tory of truth.

But as many another doctrine of the Old Testament is rendered more vivid and tangible by the
teachings of our blessed Savior, so the doctrine of
future punishment. The word employed by Him,
or rather the word used by the writers of the gos-
pels in recording in Greek His discourses, is
"Hades," invariably translated "hell" in the A.
V., except in I Cor. 15. 55, and left untranslated in
the R. V.; or the word "Gehenna," which is translated "hell" in both versions.

The former word Jesus used in His dreadful
denunciation of Capernaum : "And thou, Caper-

naum, which art exalted to heaven, shalt be thrust down to Hades ;"* and again in the parable of the rich man and Lazarus : "And in Hades he lifted up his eyes, being in torment."† If then, "Hades" is the equivalent of the " Sheol " of the Old Testament, the teachings of our Savior fix the meaning of *both* as the state of the guilty and condemned after death, and define it as a state of suffering. " I am tormented in this flame."‡ Here occurs an allusion to *fire* in this same Hades, quite in harmony with the like allusions in the Old Testament,§ and with the numerous statements of Jesus respecting future punishment.   Six times, at least, does the Lord use the burning pit *Gehenna* to represent the penal suffering of those who die in their sins.*† Elsewhere He speaks of it as "everlasting fire,"*‡ "unquenchable fire,"*§ a "furnace of fire,"** "everlasting punishment."††

It is thought by some that *Gehenna* and the other terms just quoted refer more particularly to the state or the punishment of the wicked after the final judgment—" the second death," as it is termed in Rev. xx—but it is noticeable that the same ele-

*Lu. 10. 15.   †Lu. 16. 23.   ‡Lu 16. 24.   §See Is. 33. 14; 66. 24;
   Deut. 32. 22.   *†Mat. 5. 22, 29, 30;   10. 28;   18. 9;   23. 15;
   23. 33.   *‡Mat. 18. 8;   25, 41.   *§Mk. 9. 43;   Luke. 17. 3;
**Mat. 13. 42, 50.   ††Mat. 25. 46.

ment, fire, is mentioned by Jesus in connection with *Hades.* If Hades, then, is to be limited in meaning to the state of the wicked between death and the final resurrection and judgment, we may clearly infer their state to be essentially the same, or similar, before and after that great day. Perhaps even the false hopes of the intermediate state (Lu. 16. 24, 27), will then depart forever. Except in this respect, I find no clearly marked difference denoted in Scripture.

The solicitude and suffering of Christ for the salvation of men, and the untiring zeal of the apostles for the same end after they were filled with the Spirit, can only be accounted for on the ground that hell is an awful reality, and that when once it has become the award of the wicked it is without hope. I fail to find any ground for the doctrines of Restorationism and Annihilationism. These doctrines have again and again been set aside by the church, and I do not doubt that they ever will be. Still they come up to beguile unstable souls and to try the faith of the church.

Christ on the cross, in the agony of separation from the conscious presence of the Father, has given to those who will observe and understand, the final, incontrovertible evidence of the nature of future punishment. One of the ways in which He "brought life and immortality to light," was by presenting so vividly and clearly the alternative. Can the Christian teacher do better than to accept in faith these teachings as he does the other words of his Master, and proclaim them with the same calm confidence? Is the disciple above his Master or the servant above his Lord? He may thus incur the displeasure of the world, both in the church and out of it; but in what other way can he be "clear of the blood of all men?"

APPENDIX B.

PERSONALITY AND CHARACTER OF SATAN.

IS Satan a living, intelligent, malicious person, or only an evil principle or evil disposition?

This, also, is a question of *fact*, and one which can only be conclusively settled by *testimony*. The reliable witness is the word of God. Many persons entertain speculative notions upon the subject, and hold those notions as tenaciously as if they had a right to them; while the Bible, which answers the question clearly and with authority, is not allowed a hearing at all. Some of these mistaken persons profess Christianity and a belief in the Bible; yet rest in an erroneous opinion rather than "search the Scriptures diligently to see whether these things are so." The better to enforce the testimony of our unimpeachable witness, we will preface it by a simple illustration:

Suppose that in rambling through the woods you should approach what seemed to you a large stone, and that as you draw near it should speak to you. You would be startled, of course, and would look about to find the *person* who had uttered intelligible words. You pass quite round the stone and satisfy yourself that the voice is from the stone itself, and is not an echo. It is not the voice of a bird, for it reasons with you, answers your questions, and displays original cunning. You go on your way, and presently the rough stone is in your path again. You question why it is there, and it returns an intelligent answer. You find that it has the power of voluntary motion, and that it comes there because it pleased. You are now ready to say, That which conversed with me, sometimes persuasively, sometimes angrily, but always intelligently, and which persisted in getting in my way as I walked, was not a stone, but a *person*. And if you knew that you were awake and possessed of all your faculties, the whole world could not drive you from your conclusion.

Let us see now what the Bible teaches us about Satan. First—In speaking of him, it invariably uses the masculine pronoun *he*, which, of course, implies personality, except when used figuratively. Secondly—The Bible attributes to Satan and his angels every essential attribute of a free, created personality similar to men and to other intelligent beings. Observe what these attributes are:

1—INTELLECT. Jesus "suffered not the devils to speak, because they *knew* Him. (Mark 1. 34). Here the powers of preception and comparison are unmistakably indicated. "The *wiles* of the devil," (Eph. 6. 11), represents him as having constructive imagination. James's assertion that "the devils believe" (Jas. 2. 19), attributes to them the power of *reasoning*; and so does Paul's expression, "doctrines of devils." (I. Ti. 4. 1). The three chief forms of intellectual activity are therefore present in demons, according to Scripture testimony. They are all very clearly portrayed in the account of Job and that of Christ.

2—SENSIBILITY. To Satan and other devils belongs also an emotional nature. "Art thou come to *torment* us?" (Mat. 8. 29), shows them capable of *pain*. "Devils *tremble*" (Jas. 2. 19), shows them capable of *fear*. "Ye are of your father the

devil, and the *lusts* of your father ye will do"
(John 8. 44), shows them to have *desires*. The
same is shown in Mat. 8. 31: "And the devils *besought* Him, saying, If thou cast us out, send us
away into the herd of swine."

3—WILL (Choice and Volition). *Choice* is
clearly shown in the last preceding quotation ; also
in I. Pet. 5. 8: "*Seeking* whom he may devour."
Volition is shown in the expressions, "When the
the devil *had thrown* him in the midst." (Lu. 4.
35). "The devil threw him down and tore him"
(Lu. 9. 42); and Paul's statement that some are
taken captive by the devil "at his will" (II.
Tim. 2. 26).

4—MORAL ACCOUNTABILITY. "The devil sinneth from the beginning." (I. John 3. 8). It
would be impossible for the devil to sin, unless he
had a knowledge of right and wrong, and power to
choose between them. "The devil that deceived
them was cast into the lake of fire." (Rev. 20. 10).
Here is punishment. Punishment implies guilt,
and guilt the ability to have done otherwise. Devils
are therefore *accountable* beings. If the possession
of Intellect, Sensibility and Will, the essential faculties of mind, did not prove the personality of

demons, their accountability for their conduct does prove it beyond all question.

5—SPEECH. " The devils besought." (Mat. 8:31). Satan answered the Lord and said." (Job 1. 7, 9).

6—HEARING AND UNDERSTANDING. "Get thee hence for it is written." (Mat. 4. 10). See also Job 1. 6, to 2. 7.

These plain evidences show Satan, the devil, and indeed all devils to be *created* beings; for the Uncreated is not accountable : to be *free*, because they have sinned : and to be *personalities* essentially similar to men and other intelligences.

Now note some things which the Bible does *not* teach :

1—It does not teach, anywhere, that Satan is a mere " principle of evil." If it did, it must contradict itself. A principle has none of the six personal attributes above given. Least of all, could it be accountable. To assert, therefore, that Satan is a " principle of evil," is to make God the author of sin.

2—The Bible does not teach that the devil is a human " disposition " or " tendency." A man thinks, but his disposition does not think. A man feels, but his disposition does not feel. A man wills,

and may have a willful disposition, but his disposition does not will.   He speaks, hears and understands ; but his disposition does none of these things.
He may be more or less accountable for his disposition, but his disposition is not accountable.

3—For like reasons, it is clear that the Bible
does not teach that the devil is a disease or infirmity, or that diseases and infirmities are devils.

4—The Bible does not teach that " every man
is his own devil."   How absurd is such a thought
in the light of Scripture statement.   " I beheld
Satan as lightning fall from heaven." (Lu. 10.
18).   " Satan hath desired to have you." (Lu. 22.
31).   " Out of whom He had cast seven devils."
(Mk. 16. 9).   " When the unclean spirit is gone out
of a man, etc." (Mat. 12. 43).   " Then went the
devils out of the man." (Lu. 8. 33).   " The devil
leaveth him." (Mat. 4. 11).

When Christ said to Peter, " Get thee behind
me Satan," He evidently rebuked Peter as the temporary though unconscious representative of Satan
in the statement he had just made ; or perhaps the
word Satan was used in its ordinary signification of
adversary.   When He said to the disciples, " One
of you is a devil," He merely announced beforehand the completeness of Judas' apostasy, and his

becoming one in purpose, character and doom with the kingdom of Satan.

While Satan is, in power and in cunning, superhuman, as we are bound to infer from the Scripture testimony, he is not omnipresent. He is not in heaven and never will be. (Rev. 21. 27 ; 20. 10). His apparent ubiquity is due to the fact that he has numerous messengers who are one in nature, character and purpose with himself, and thus every man is tempted by him through these messengers. He is not omniscient, nor omnipotent. Though he is a malignant personal enemy of God and of our souls, the soul that is cleansed by the precious blood of Christ and remains fully committed to Him, has nothing to fear from this fallen angel. On the contrary, Satan's snares and wiles, discovered and resisted in the power of the Holy Spirit, who is always present with the trusting and obedient believer, become a means of added knowledge, strength and faith; and so are among the "all things" that "work together for good to them that love God, to them that are the called according to His purpose." Such have always had the victory through Him that loved us and gave Himself for us. "They overcame him by the blood of the Lamb and by the word of their testimony."

APPENDIX C.

DIVINE WRATH.

THE thought that anger, indignation or wrath exists in the mind of God, is extremely distasteful to some, who deem it incompatible with other attributes ascribed to Him in the Scriptures, and even with His own demands upon men. It is indeed remarkable that the frequent use, in Scripture, of those expressions which attribute such emotions to Deity, has been repeatedly urged as an argument against the inspiration of the Bible, by those whose contrary notion of Divine purity, holiness and love has been received, either directly or indirectly, from the Bible alone.

Christians have often been puzzled to explain these expressions, and some religious teachers have offered explanations little calculated to promote confidence in the Book. One writer boldly asserts "God never was angry;" thus opposing his own opinion to much positive Scripture statement.

The difficulty with such persons is this: They conceive of anger only as it is exhibited by depraved humanity; and as thus exhibited they deem it essentially and utterly contrary to virtue and love. The opinion thus formed is held as sacred truth, and even the word of God is judged by it. The error of such persons would be quickly dispelled by looking beneath the surface of things, and discovering the true nature of that which they so hastily condemn.

Whether in its milder form, to which we give the name of indignation, or in its more destructive form, in which we speak of it as wrath, anger is, in its true *nature*, as pure and innocent as any other emotion. As it is impossible to form any true conception of a rational, moral being, even of God Himself, which does not embrace an emotional nature, so it is impossible to conceive of any just administration of government among free moral and sinful beings, in which this particular emotion is not exercised.

A moral government in which guilt is not followed by condemnation and penalty, is a myth or a mockery. In all pure minds the perception of injustice is followed by a sense (an emotion) of repugnance, the expression of which, through the moral judgment, is condemnation. But in such minds there arises also another emotion, the expression of which, through the will, is punishment. That emotion is called anger, indignation, or wrath, according to its real or supposed intensity ; though these terms are often used indiscriminately, or without reference to degrees of intensity. Probably all persons who have seriously thought upon the subject, believe in such a thing as just indignation. Who would wish to be the parent of a boy who could listen to a story of cruelty and outrage, and not have his eye glisten and his face burn with an impulse to right the wrong and bring the offender to justice? Or what son would delight to own a parent who was incapable of such emotion, or who failed judiciously to manifest it?

But lest these remarks should seem to excuse the irritability and the tempestuous passion which, instead of promoting, go so far to disturb the peace of the home and of society, it is necessary to distinguish between the *nature* of an emotion and its *exercise*, and between its moral and its sinful exercise—its use and its abuse. No impurity can be charged against any of the natural appetites, as to its nature; nor does guilt attach to its proper use; but any of these, when exercised beyond the limits of its true purpose, or upon improper objects, or contrary to the will of God, becomes sinful. The same is true of the desires and affections.

The true purpose of anger (using this term in its generic sense) is the defense of right against wrong by the punishment of sin. But just as the innocent appetite of hunger, in a depraved being and under temptation, leads to gluttony, or the appetite of thirst to drunkenness; as the desire of esteem leads to ambition, and the desire of possession to covetousness; so the emotion of anger, in its appointed sphere one of the marks of noble mind, becomes in fallen man a source of untold wrong and suffering. It rises and finds expression in words, looks and actions before the mind has received any proper evidence of injustice; it is called forth by mere suspicion; it is excessive in its awards; it rises to passion and for the time dethrones reason; it deranges the functions of mind and body; it even usurps the Divine authority, inflicting punishments which none but God has the right to inflict.

It is in such unholy and debasing exercise of it, that human anger is so strongly condemned in the Bible. And it is this view of it which has caused some to deny its existence in the Divine mind. Anger is, however, in its nature, a moral emotion, and in an omniscient and holy being is never exercised against the innocent, nor beyond the limit of perfect justice. It does not antagonize nor obscure any other attribute of the Divine nature. When we read that "the anger of the Lord was kindled against Balaam;" that "God is angry with the

wicked every day ;" " the indignation of the Lord
is upon all nations ;" " the wrath of God is revealed
from heaven against all unrighteousness," etc.; we
are not to think of that malignant, passionate state
of mind which so often saddens us when we view
ourselves or our fellow men, but simply of that
movement of the emotional nature toward the execution of justice, which is essential to the moral
government of the universe, to the holiness of God,
and not less essential to His love.

An eminent writer has said, " When God is displeased with the sinner, he compassionately desires
that the sinner may escape the displeasure, and in-
vents a way of escaping it.   But when man is displeased with his fellow man, he does not desire that
his fellow man may escape the displeasure, and
devises no way of escape."

It should be noted that in some cases in the
Bible the terms wrath and anger, as applied to God,
are employed to denote not merely emotion—perhaps not this at all—but rather judgment, condemnation or punishment. " The wrath of God abideth
on him." " [We] were by nature children of
wrath."   Several other Bible expressions illustrate
this use of the term.

With the foregoing explanations, such expressions as we find in the Bible respecting Divine anger cannot awaken unpleasant thoughts of God, except, perhaps, in the minds of those who have occasion to dread His justice, and are unwilling to accept His mercy.

There is scarcely an evidence of human depravity more striking than the well-nigh universal abuse of the emotion of anger, resulting in the very injustice and cruelty which it was designed to correct. Because of this abuse, the apostle could correctly say, " The wrath of man worketh not the righteousness of God." There is scarcely a more satisfactory mark of the triumph of grace in the soul, than the habitual restraint of this emotion to the limits of its true purpose. " He that subdueth anger, is better than the mighty; and he that ruleth his spirit than he that taketh a city."

APPENDIX D.

IMMORTALITY.

THAT all men, regardless of their relation to salvation, have souls which live and exercise the powers of thought, feeling and volition, even when separated from the body; and that these souls continue to exist, and to exercise their powers forever, has been the belief of the church in all ages. This belief rests upon plain Scripture statement.

That there is a soul distinct from the body, and capable of existing apart from it is taught in such passages as the following :

I. Ki. 17. 21, 22. "And he stretched himself upon the child three times, and cried unto the Lord and said, O Lord, my God, I pray thee let this child's soul come into him again ; and the Lord heard the voice of Elijah ; and the soul of the child came into him again, and he revived."

Micah 6. 7. "Shall I give * * the fruit of my body for the sin of my soul ?"

Mat. 10. 28. "Fear not them which kill the body but are not able to kill the soul."

Lu. 8. 55. "And her spirit came again, and she arose."

Lu. 24. 37, 39. "They supposed they had seen a spirit." "A spirit hath not flesh and bones as ye see me have."

Acts 7. 59. "Lord Jesus, receive my spirit."

II. Cor. 4. 16. "For though our outward man perish, the inward man is renewed day by day."

II. Cor. 5. 8. "We are confident, and willing rather to be absent from the body, and to be present with the Lord."

II. Cor. 12. 2. "Whether in the body or out of the body I cannot tell."

Apart, therefore, from the evidences of natural religion and of science, which the Christian world has regarded as supporting the doctrine of our two-fold nature (and never more confidently than at present), the above passages and many others have furnished a basis of belief, firm and impregnable because a part of the Divine revelation.

Upon like evidence Christians have also confidently affirmed the soul's eternal conscious existence. Dan. 12. 3. "And they that be wise shall shine with the brightness of the firmament; and they that turn many to righteousness as the stars forever and ever."

Mat. 22. 32. "God is not the God of the dead but of the living." (Yet those to whom Jesus had just referred had long been dead physically.)

Mat. 17. 3. "And behold there appeared unto them Moses and Elias, talking with them."

Lu. 16. 22, etc. (The account of the rich man and Lazarus.)

Lu. 18. 30. "In the world to come, life ever-lasting."

John 10. 28. "I give unto them eternal life, and

they shall never perish, neither shall any man pluck them out of my hand."

Rev. 3 12.   "Him that overcometh will I make a pillar in the temple of my God, and he shall go no more out."

I. Thess. 4. 17. "And so shall we ever be with the Lord."

Rev. 22. 5.   "And they shall reign forever and ever."

Statements like these, occurring frequently in the Holy Scriptures, are conclusive evidence of the endless life of the righteous.   They of course embrace much more than the idea of endless consciousness, for they include that peculiar form of life, or state of the soul, which is the result of personal salvation.   But they none the less clearly include the lower idea of endless consciousness.

What is the testimony of the inspired record respecting the endless consciousness of the wicked ? This has already been set forth in Appendix A, of this volume, and references will not be repeated here.   Those references have been regarded as conclusive by Christians generally.   Some persons are disposed to set them aside for this or that reason ; but as yet no very satisfactory argument is offered. The strongest is that which is based upon certain texts that seem to teach the opposite idea, that the finally impenitent will cease to exist.

"Yet a little while and the wicked shall not be." Ps. 37. 10, 11. "In that very day their thoughts perish." Ps. 146. 4. "There is no work, nor device, nor knowledge, nor wisdom in the grave." Eccl. 9. 10. "The enemies of the Lord shall be as the fat of lambs; they shall consume; into smoke shall they consume away." Ps. 37. 19, 20. "All the proud, yea and all that do wickedly, shall be stubble, and the day that cometh shall burn them up * * that it shall leave them neither root nor branch." Mal. 4. 1.

Of texts like these there is a considerable number; and apart from the setting in which they occur, or the evident design of the writer, they might have great weight against the doctrine of universal immortality. But upon careful examination and comparison they are found to have little if any bearing upon that doctrine.

Take the above quotations. "Yet a little while and the wicked shall not be." This and similar expressions in the same psalm would be strictly appropriate to the thought of the composer, if he had in mind only the fact that as a rule righteous men far *outlive* wicked men. They would also be appropriate if he had reference to the final triumph of righteousness on the earth. In either case the next statement, "Thou shalt diligently consider his place and it shall not be," would denote only the place of the wicked *on earth.* The wicked shall not exist *on earth;* they shall die and be seen no more. No man, therefore, can safely assert that these expressions have any reference at all to the soul, or to the ultimate extinction of a portion of the human race.

"In that very day his thoughts perish." More fully, "Put not your trust in princes, nor in the son of man, in whom there is no help. His breath goeth forth, he returneth to his earth; in that very day his thoughts perish." Here no distinction is made between the righteous and the wicked. The statement includes all mankind. If used to prove the extinction of the wicked, it will equally prove the extinction of the just. Evidently it has no reference to the extinction of either. "His thoughts perish," simply means that at death his planning and scheming respecting earthly things are at an end, and he cannot be thy permanent helper.

"There is no work, nor device, nor knowledge, nor wisdom in the grave." This is a universal statement, applying equally to the righteous and the wicked. If it affirms extinction or an inactive and unconscious state of the wicked, it affirms the same for the righteous. But the Bible makes clear the continued activity and consciousness of the righteous after death. Hence this passage cannot be justly taken as proving the opposite even for the wicked. A glance at the context plainly shows that it refers solely to earthly affairs, all human control of which ceases at the grave.

"The enemies of the Lord shall be as the fat of lambs; they shall consume; into smoke shall they consume away." If we could *know* that this text was intended to refer to cessation of soul life, it might seem very conclusive; but when we read the verse which precedes it, we find it to be merely a promise that "in the days of famine" there shall be a difference between the righteous and the wicked, the latter perishing while the former are preserved.

The text from Malachi, "All the proud and all that do wickedly shall be stubble," etc., is by no means necessarily to receive a literal interpretation. It certainly indicates the ultimate triumph of righteousness and extinction of wickedness in the earth, or at least in the Jewish nation to which it is addressed. The passage is highly figurative, and evidently so. Probably no one thinks that the wicked will be literally transformed into "stubble," or that they have roots and branches; nor is it probable that the "ashes" and the burning are here intended to denote a purely physical phenomenon and its result. The prophecy lacks the perfect clearness which characterizes the teachings of the Savior in relation to the final state of the wicked; and to insist upon its denoting the final extinction of the wicked, body and soul, is not only to do violence to the just principles of interpretation, but to make it contradict or interpret the teachings of our blessed Lord, either of which would be an error.

These examples illustrate the danger of relying upon isolated texts, however numerous they may be; since every one of them, rightly understood, may embody a very different thought from what it seemed at first to convey.

It is very significant that the immortality of the soul, though questioned by materialists of every age, has been uniformly held by Christian scholars, with very few exceptions. The endless conscious existence of the righteous no Christian seems to wish to call in question. Some do question that of the wicked. But the chief authority for both is the Bible. To question either is to question the authority of the Scriptures.   To reject either is to reject that authority, and exalt in its place the reason of men.   Alas for such trifling with the great concerns of eternity !

NOTE.—The word immortality is here used in its popular sense, as denoting endless conscious existence.   Some persons use it as denoting death-lessness in every sense, whether physical or spirit-ual.   In this sense no human being can be called immortal until after the resurrection and judg-ment; and then only the righteous; for then the wicked will be in the state of spiritual death as defined in Chapter III. of this volume.   In this sense also Christ Himself was not immortal until after His resurrection.   This use of the words "immortal" and "immortality" may be quite ad-admissible, but I have not thought it needful to adopt it.

APPENDIX E.

TOTAL DEPRAVITY AND ORIGINAL SIN.

PERHAPS the Scriptural evidences of the state of man in the fall, apart from the gracious work of redemption, have been sufficiently set forth in the early chapters of this volume ; but I wish to group them here for easy reference, and show the propriety or impropriety of the above terms, and the doctrines denoted by them.

The Bible clearly teaches that in the fall man lost the Divine image in which he had been created. " Them He did predestinate to be conformed to the image of His Son." Rom. 8. 29. " As we have borne the image of the earthy, we shall also bear the image of the heavenly." I. Cor. 15. 49. " But we all with open face [believers are addressed] beholding as in a glass the glory of the Lord, are changed to the same image from glory to glory as by the Spirit of the Lord." II. Cor. 3. 18. " Ye have put on the new man which is renewed in knowledge after the image of Him that created him." Col. 3. 10. " I shall be satisfied, when I awake, with thy likeness." Ps. 17. 15. "Be ye not conformed to this world, but be ye transformed by the renewing of your mind." Rom. 12. 2.

If the work of redemption is to bring believers into the likeness of the Son, who is the express image of the Father's person (Heb. 1. 3), it is beyond all doubt that in the fall man *lost* that image, and that the unconverted do not bear that image. Its restoration begins, to the sinner, in regeneration. "If any man be in Christ, he is a new creature." II.

Cor. 5. 17. It is complete in the resurrection. "Beloved, now are we the sons of God, and it doth not yet appear what we shall be; but we know that when He shall appear we shall be like Him; for we shall see Him as he is." I. John 3. 2. Those, therefore, who assert that the Divine image was not lost when the penalty of death was visited upon the transgressor, contradict the plain teachings of the inspired record.

Observe the following Bible description of man apart from grace: "What then, are we better than they? No, in no wise : for we have before proved both Jews and Gentiles, that they are all under sin; As it is written, There is none righteous, no, not one: there is none that understandeth, there is none that seeketh after God. They are all gone out of the way, they are together become unprofitable; there is none that doeth good, no, not one." Thus far the negative description, now the positive. "Their throat is an open scpulcher; with their tongues they have used deceit; the poison of asps is under their lips; Whose mouth is full of cursing and bitterness; Their feet are swift to shed blood : Destruction and misery are in their ways; And the way of peace have they not known : There is no fear of God before their eyes. Now we know that whatsoever things the law saith, it saith to them who are under the law, that every mouth may be stopped, and all the world may become guilty before God." Rom. 3. 9-19.

This is a most melancholy picture of the state of death, which is the wages of sin. But "*it is written*," and cannot pass away. It clearly represents the unregenerate as neither able nor inclined to seek God ; and this charge is confirmed beyond all doubt by the words of our blessed Savior : " No man cometh unto the Father but *by me ; and no man cometh unto me, except the Father which hath sent me draw him.*" John 14. 6; 6. 44. The statement of Paul (I. Cor. 2 14), as positively asserts the same truth in another aspect of it : "The natural man receiveth not the things of the spirit of God ; for they are foolishness unto him ; neither can he know them, because they are spiritually discerned." By the "natural man," Paul means not the "animal man" as some have imagined, but the whole man, rational, intelligent, but considered in himself alone, apart from the effectual work of redemption. Paul frequently uses " the flesh " in the same sense. " In me, that is, in my flesh, dwelleth no good thing." Rom. 7. 18. " They that are in the flesh cannot please God." Rom. 8. 8. " The flesh lusteth against the Spirit." Gal. 5. 17. "The works of the flesh are manifest, which are adultery, fornication, uncleanness, lasciviousness, idolatry, witchcraft, hatred, variance, emulations, wrath, strife, seditions, heresies, envyings, murders, drunkenness, revellings, and such like." Gal. 5. 19. In which of these works does a man resemble God? Or which of them is a movement toward God? It is needless to add anything more to prove that the sinner is neither able nor inclined to seek God or to keep His law by virtue of anything which belongs to him as a child of Adam, a natural man.

How then do we account for so much that is commendable and even lovely in some persons who are unconverted? "I, if I be lifted up from the earth, will draw all men unto me." John 12. 32. This explains it, and it is *God's* explanation. But it has been so fully presented in Chapters XVII, XVIII, that we will not repeat here the proofs, but only reaffirm that whatever godliness or goodness there is in any man is the result of the Savior's work for him.

The Society of Friends, and some other evangelical Christians discard the term "total depravity;" not because it does not properly express the hopeless, helpless state of the sinner, when consid-

ered apart from the blessings of redemption ; for
the term is no stronger than the statements of Scripture fully warrant : but because those who use the
term apply it (or seem to apply it) to persons in
whom some of the influences of grace are yet efficient.   Any such application is unjust toward God.
If Paul had said, " I know that in me dwelleth no
good thing," he would have denied the work of
grace in him.   He would also have dishonored the
Holy Ghost ; for he himself taught that the Christian is the temple of God.(I. Cor. 3. 16, 17; 6. 19.)
But Paul carefully guards this point by saying, " I
know that in me, *that is*, *in my flesh*," the natural
man considered apart from the work of grace,
"dwelleth no good thing."   If those who use the
term "total depravity" were as careful in limiting
its application, its use might be quite unobjection-
able.   But to apply it without qualification to infants,
in whom (as we have shown in Chapter XVII),
the unconditional benefits of the Atonement are
operative, or even to the unrepentant sinner, in
whom some of these may yet remain in some degree
operative, is to misrepresent both God and man.
To represent man as having in himself, by nature,
any power or disposition to please God, would be
utterly contrary to the Divine word.   On the other

hand, to deny that all men, in virtue of the work of Christ for them, and of the Holy Ghost within them, have power to choose life, to come to repentance, to believe and be saved, is to dishonor Father, Son and Holy Spirit, and the teachings and invitations of Scripture.   Both errors should be carefully avoided.

As to " original sin," the Bible teaches that the posterity of Adam were and are by nature like their fallen parent   Gen. 5. 3 "Adam   *   *   begat a son in his own likeness, after his image."   This was *fallen* Adam, who, as we have just shown, was no longer in the image of God.

The question may be asked, Had not Adam by this time exercised saving faith and become regenerate , and if so would not his offspring have spiritual life by natural law ?   Or, may not Adam have become a thoroughly sanctified man, and if so, would not his sons who were born after this, be not only spiritually alive, but holy ?   The answer to both these questions must be negative.   " The GIFT of God is eternal life by Jesus Christ our Lord." Rom. 6. 23.   " By grace are ye saved, through faith, and that not of yourselves, it is the GIFT OF GOD." Eph. 2. 8.   Salvation, which includes life from the dead, is the direct gift of God in every instance ;

He has never made man the medium of its impartation, by heredity or otherwise. " Look unto *me*, and be ye saved, all the ends of the earth, for I am God, and there is none else." Is. 45. 22. " Neither is there salvation *in any other*." Acts 4. 12.

Every child inherits, by nature, a strong tendency, or disposition toward sin. If the term " original sin " meant nothing more than this, it would be an allowable expression. But it usually indicates also that every child is *guilty* and *under condemnation* because of Adam's sin. This we have shown (Chapters V. and XVII.) not to be the teaching of Scripture. Since the term, then, usually carries with it an unscriptural idea, Friends and some other evangelical Christians have discarded it altogether. They do not claim that the infant is inwardly and perfectly holy, though to it is imparted, as a gift from God through Christ, a measure of spiritual life. There is the inherited disposition to sin—the indwelling sin of Romans 7th—to be destroyed by the baptism with the Holy Ghost and fire. Yet the infant is not guilty and condemned, but alive, and thus far saved, as a necessary result of the Atonement. When the child reaches the age of understanding and accountability, and transgresses known law, he comes at once under condemnation and penalty as did Adam.   The doctrine of original sin, as embracing the guilt of infants and the damnation of any such as die in infancy, is, let us hope, a thing of the past.

APPENDIX F.

THE DIVINE FATHERHOOD.

THE assumption that the Fatherhood of God extends over the entire human family, regardless of their spiritual state, has led to such gross misconceptions of the Divine character, of human character, of the Holy Scriptures, and of the doctrines of Christianity, that it seems proper here to call attention to it, and to show in how far it has any Scriptural foundation.   The Bible student may observe:

1—That a very small number of texts seem to teach, plainly and purposely, the universal Divine Fatherhood. "As certain also of your own poets have said, For we are also His offspring. Forasmuch, then, as we are the offspring of God, " etc. Acts 17. 28 29. "One God and Father of all, who is over all, and through all, and in all." Eph. 4. 6.

2—That a few texts represent the Israelitish nation as a son, God being its Father. See Is. 63. 16; Jer. 3. 19, 22; 31. 9; Mal. 1. 6.

3—That the New Testament, in its manifold

allusions to the Fatherhood of God, in those cases where the words " our Father " and " your Father " are used, contemplates believers only, these being the classes addressed.   See Jesus' own use of these expressions, twenty times in Matthew, two in Mark, four in Luke, and one in John.   The apostles use the same twenty-one times in the epistles, always referring to believers.

4—That Jesus emphatically denies the claim of the unbelieving Jews, that God was their Father. " If God were your Father, ye would love me." " Ye are of your father, the Devil, and the lusts of your father ye will do."   " He that is of God, hear-eth God's words; ye therefore hear them not, because ye are not of God."   See Jno. 8. 41–49. Compare I. Jno. 3. 8,   " He that committeth sin is of the Devil; Acts 13. 10,   " O, full of all subtilty and all mischief, thou child of the Devil;" and Mat. 13. 38, " The tares are the children of the Wicked One."

5—That the gospel is an invitation to those who are in the kingdom and fatherhood of the Evil One to abandon this for the kingdom and Father-hood of God.   " Come out from among them, and be ye separate, and touch not the unclean thing, and I will receive you, and will be a Father unto you, and ye shall be my sons and daughters, saith the Lord Almighty." II. Cor. 6. 17, 18. "As many as received Him, to them gave He power to become the sons of God, even to them that believe on His name." John 1. 12. "Behold what manner of love the Father hath bestowed upon us, that we should be called the sons of God; therefore the world knoweth us not, because it knew Him not." I. Jno. 3. 1. "As many as are led by the Spirit of God, they are the sons of God." Rom. 8. 14. "Except a man be born from above, he shall not see the kingdom of God." John 3. 3.

A careful examination brings us to these conclusions:

1—That in the sense of Creator, Provider and Upholder, God is the Father of all men.

2—That it is not in this sense that Jesus speaks of His Fatherhood, but in a very different and a higher sense, denoting spiritual likeness and union, through spiritual life.

3—That this likeness and union existed in Adam before the fall, and hence he is said to have been a son of God. Lu. 3. 38.

4—That infants, because of the atonement, have, in a degree at least, this likeness and union, and thus hold, through Christ, a filial relation to God.

5—That when one has become "dead through trespasses," the life, likeness and union which form the ground of this filial relation with God, are *gone*, and that the sinner cannot truthfully call God his Father in the Gospel sense, except by being "born again," through "repentance toward God and faith in our Lord Jesus Christ."

These conclusions being fully sustained by the teachings of Scripture, it is clear that any system of religious belief based upon the universal and equal Fatherhood of God over saint and sinner, rests upon a false foundation. It is also evident that a man or woman who has not exercised repentance toward God and faith in our Lord Jesus Christ, and who nevertheless looks for salvation because God is his Father, is under a delusion. But thousands are yet in this condition ; and thousands of sinners resting in this false assumption, claim to trust in God, while walking in their own lusts. "God is not the God of the dead, but of the living ; " and His word to sinners is, "Return unto me and live."

May those who attempt to declare the gospel, observe and follow its plain teachings upon this important subject, and not lull, by false hopes, those whom they are expected to awaken and save.

The love of God is all the more wonderful and soul-tendering when this subject is viewed in its Scriptural aspect.

APPENDIX G.

THREE IN ONE.

HERE again is a question of *fact*, in which reason can be of little value, but on which we have the plain testimony of the inspired record.

1—Father, Son and Holy Spirit are distinctly spoken of, as if each were a distinct personality.

"And Jesus, when He was baptized, went up straightway out of the water; and lo, the heavens were opened unto Him, and He saw the Spirit of God descending like a dove, and lighting upon Him; and lo, a voice from heaven, saying, This is my beloved Son, in whom I am well pleased."* "Go ye therefore, and teach all nations, baptizing them in the name of the Father, and of the Son, and of the Holy Ghost."† "But the Comforter, the Holy Ghost, whom the Father will send in my name, He shall teach you all things, and bring all things to

---

*Mat. 3. 16, 17. See also Mk. 1. 9-11; Lu. 3. 21, 22; John 1. 32-34. †Mat. 28. 19.

your remembrance, whatsoever I have said unto you."*   "The grace of the Lord Jesus Christ, and the love of God, and the communion of the Holy Ghost, be with you all."†   "For through Him we both have access, by one Spirit, unto the Father."‡ "Christ, who through the eternal Spirit, offered Himself without spot to God,"§ etc.

2—All the essential attributes of a distinct personality are applied to each—Intellect, Sensibility, Will, Freedom, Power, Expression.   It is said of

The Father,	The Son,	The Holy Spirit,
"God saw that it was good." Gen. 1. 10.	"Jesus knew their thoughts." Mat. 12. 25.	"He shall testify of me." John 15. 26.
"God so loved the world." John 3. 16.	"When Jesus saw it, He was much displeased." Mk. 10. 14.	"For the love of the Spirit." Rom. 15. 30.
"He hath done whatsoever He hath pleased." Ps. 115. 3.	"Jesus did not commit Himself unto them, because He knew all men." John 2. 24.	"Maketh intercession for us." Rom. 8. 26. "Helpeth our infirmities." (ib.) "The power of the Holy Ghost." Rom. 15. 13.
"God created the heavens and the earth." Gen. 1. 1.	"By whom are all things." 1. Cor. 8. 6.	"The Spirit speaketh expressly." 1 Tim. 4. 1.
"God said, Let there be light." Gen. 1. 3.	"Jesus said unto Him." Mat. 4. 7.	"Dividing to every man severally as He will." 1 Cor. 12. 11.

These illustrative texts (a few out of many), clearly show the truth of the above proposition.

---

*John 14. 26; see John 15. 26. †2 Cor. 13. 14. ‡Eph. 2. 18. §Heb. 9. 14.

3—To each of the three are ascribed the same Divine character and attributes.

	To Father.	To Son.	To Holy Ghost.
Omnipresence..	Eph. 1. 23.	Mat. 18. 20.	1 Cor. 3. 16.
Omniscience ...	Acts 1. 24.	John 6. 64.	1 Cor. 2. 10.
Omnipotence...	Mat. 19. 26.	Heb. 1. 3.	1 Cor. 12. 4-11.
Eternity	1 Tim. 1. 17.	Col. 1. 17.	Heb. 9. 14.
Holiness.........	Mat. 19. 17.	Mk. 1. 24.	His title.
Goodness........	James 1. 17.	Acts 10. 38.	Ps. 143. 10.
Creative power	Gen. 1. 27.	Heb. 1. 2.	Job 33. 4.

4—It is distinctly declared that there is one God, and that these three are One.

"There is none other God but one." 1 Cor. 8. 4.

"Hear, O Israel, the Lord our God is one Lord." Deut. 6. 4.

"One God and Father of all, who is above all, and through all, and in all." Ep. 4. 6.

"Thou believest that there is one God; thou doest well." James 2. 19.

"There are three that bear record in heaven, the Father, the Word, and the Holy Ghost, and these three are one." 1 John 5. 7.

Since all of these four points are the subject of direct Scripture testimony, all are to be fully accepted as true—the personality, the distinctness, the equality, the oneness.

How the three are one, the Scripture leaves unexplained; and many a serious error has resulted from the attempts of men to resolve the mystery.

Some have said that " there is but one Person, man-
ifesting Himself in three influences, operations or
offices." Such a belief does away the personality
of the Son and the Holy Spirit, and thus does violence to the plain and oft-repeated testimony of
Scripture. Some have partly avoided this last
difficulty by attributing personality and Godhead to
Jesus Christ, as the One God, thus doing away the
personality of the Father and the Holy Spirit.
Some have boldly made the Son and the Holy
Ghost created and subordinate beings. To some
the proper view of the subject, which honors all
Bible testimony and rejects none, is this: that
Father, Son and Holy Spirit are distinct personalities, yet so essentially the same in nature and attributes, character and purpose, that it cannot possibly
be said that there are three Gods. This view honors
the Son even as it honors the Father,* and does not
degrade the Holy Spirit to be a mere influence or
emanation from God. It becomes, moreover, a most
precious and helpful doctrine to the true believer,
ministering to tenderness, gentleness and love, and
to all the Christian graces. Yet even this view presents difficulties to the mind, and we are fain to
leave the matter where the Gospel leaves it, believ-

---

*John 5. 22, 23.

ing fully the personality and yet the oneness of Father, Son and Holy Ghost. I quote from Dougan Clark the words of Mansell, " We know that God is three in one because that is revealed. We do not know *how* He is three in one, because that is not revealed, and we can know it in no other way."

APPENDIX H.

AN EARLY REVELATION.

THE identity of human nature from age to age, the nature of salvation, the unchanging love of God, and the fact that the fall took place in our first parents, form strong presumptive evidence of a clear, early revelation of the plan of salvation. Salvation is essentially the same in pauper and prince, in the savage and the sage. There is but *one way* of salvation, repentance toward God and faith in our Lord Jesus Christ. Salvation may, it is true, take place upon widely different moral and intellectual planes; otherwise it could not be offered to all. But in every case of a sinner's being saved there is the knowledge of sin, the sense of condemnation for sin, the desire for deliverance, the turning from sin and self to seek after God, and the faith which lays hold on God's appointed means, even in the absence of any true conception of what that means is.   If Adam, Eve, Abel, Seth, Enoch, Abraham, became children of God after transgression, all these conditions must have been present; and to their longing souls God must, in consideration of His purpose in Christ, have given conceptions of that purpose, sufficiently clear to serve as an incentive to hope, and a ground of faith.   Happily we have much more than presumptive evidence upon this interesting theme.

Some writers upon religion are so fully committed to the idea of evolution, that they assume, or assert, the various religions of the world to have been so many links in a complete chain of evolution, Christianity being the latest, and *thus far the highest*.   Such writers appear to assume the feebleness and ignorance of the race in earliest times, and forget that "there were giants in the earth in those days," intellectual giants, moral giants, spiritual giants, as well as physical giants.

It will not do to liken the early inhabitants of the world to the benighted savages of our day. These, through the unfaithfulness of their more favored brethren or their ancestors, are destitute of light which the ante-diluvian world, in the very nature of things, must have possessed, and which we have proof that it did possess.   Before the flood

the one great transaction of history was the fall.
This was no myth, but a tremendous reality. Of
its awful significance, no doubt those who suffered
it had a very clear apprehension. A striking evidence of this is found in the sad, though selfish
complaint of Cain, "And from thy face shall I be
hid." Here is set forth with unmistakable clearness the essential character of the Divinely appointed penalty for transgression. [See Gen. 4. 14].
The sad story of the fall must have been handed
down, with solemn interest, from age to age. Adam
himself lived to tell it to Lamech through 86 years
of the latter's boyhood; and Lamech was the father
of Noah.

But along with this melancholy story went a
very different one, the story of a promised redemption. Worship was taught and practised. A ritual
accompanied it—the offering of sacrifice with blood.
In Genesis, the record of the first sixteen centuries
is embraced in six brief chapters. One of these is
devoted to the fall, the promise of a victorious
Savior, and an adequate covering provided for the
sinning pair. Is it too much to believe that with
the promise of a Savior there came clear light on
the means of redemption and the manner of it? Is
it too much to believe that the "coats of skins,"

taken from slain beasts, were designed to teach and did teach those first sinners that they could only be shielded from Divine punishment by the death of another for them? Is it too much to believe that just here God laid the foundation of the system of expiatory sacrifice, a type by which the suffering of the Son of God should be kept in remembrance until He should be visibly offered up?

In Genesis 4th chapter we mark the name of Eve's first-born son, "Gotten," for this is what "Cain" signifies. One naturally suspects that, with the promise of a Savior still running in her mind, she thought of her son as the fulfillment of that promise. Be that as it may, we cannot read the following story of Cain's and Abel's offerings without being impressed with the responsibility of these two men for the character of their offerings. This responsibility must have rested upon *previous enlightenment.* The Lord's reproof of Cain, "If thou doest well, shalt thou not be accepted?" is followed by a most loving suggestion of the means of grace: "And if thou doest not well, a sin offering coucheth at the door; and its desire shall be to thee, but thou shalt rule over it." The whole transaction, and these wonderful words, must have been big with meaning to those two brethren.

Expiation is plainly taught in the book of Job, which is older than the Mosaic law. It is taught in the story of Balak and Balaam, which is as old as the fourth book of the Pentateuch. It was taught nearly five centuries earlier by Abraham to Isaac. It has been taught in heathen nations generally.

Side by side with this important though often gravely misapprehended doctrine, has been that of salvation by a Messiah—a personal, superhuman character to come. Worldly men have looked for a deliverer of their nation or tribe from the power of other nations or tribes. Devout men have looked for a Savior from the penal consequences of sin, and from the power of sin.

But the New Testament affords, perhaps, the clearest evidence of an early revelation. Our Savior attributes to Abraham a clear knowledge of His coming and His work when He says, "Abraham rejoiced to see my day, and he saw it and was glad." To say that Abraham foresaw our Savior only as " the promised Seed " in whom the families of the earth should be [in some way] blessed, and not as the Lamb of God, whose sacrifice should be the atonement for sin, would be a great injustice. For our Savior, in speaking of His office as the

Messiah, always had in mind His suffering for the sins of the world as a sacrifice appointed and accepted by the Father. See Jno. 3. 14, 15; 8. 28; 12. 32, and many others. The Holy Ghost, by the mouth of Peter, in the clearest, strongest manner, attributes to David a foreknowledge of the great transaction. See Acts 2. 25–35.

The writer of the Epistle to the Hebrews gives unmistakable testimony to the same knowledge on the part of the holy men of earlier times, beginning his list with Abel (Heb. 11.). After naming Enoch, Noah, Abraham and Sarah, he says, "These all died in faith." These and the persons mentioned later in the chapter, the writer evidently regarded as saints, saved by grace through faith. His testimony on this point is clear. But he also regarded saving faith as including *more* than the incipient faith which he mentions in verse 6: "He that cometh to God must first believe that He is, and that He is a rewarder of them that diligently seek Him." "Believe on the Lord Jesus Christ, and thou shalt be saved," was Paul's own word to the Philippian jailer. To him the faith which brings justification, is faith in the Lord Jesus Christ "sacrificed for us." He teaches no other doctrine as applicable to any age; and here, in the epistle

to the Hebrews, where this doctrine is made very clear, he affirms of these holy men of old, that they had not received the promises (that is, in fulfillment), but that they had "seen them afar off and were persuaded of them and embraced them."*
Peter bears similar testimony (I. Pet. 1. 10, 11) where he says, "Of which salvation the prophets have inquired and searched diligently, who prophesied of the grace that should come unto you; searching what, or what manner of time the Spirit of Christ which was in them did signify, when it testified beforehand the sufferings of Christ, and the glory that should follow." These apostles, like the prophets of old, "spake as they were moved by the Holy Ghost." Their testimony is, therefore, unimpeachable and conclusive, as to an early, clear revelation of the plan of redemption in all its essential features. It is only with reference to the unfolding of its circumstances, time, place and other historic relations, that the idea of evolution can be properly applied to the plan of redemption; and this is a question of relatively little importance.

---

*Paul may not have been the author of this epistle; but the teachings contained in it are Pauline throughout.

APPENDIX I.

DIVINE PASSIBILITY.

PASSIBILITY is the capability of feeling or suffering. The question is raised, "Could Deity suffer?" Unbelief blindly asserts that if Christ is God, as Christians affirm, and if Christ died, then God was dead, and the universe was for a time without a governor.

The foolishness of such reasoning appears, when we consider that Christians also affirm Christ to be God the Son ; that at His death He commended His spirit to God the Father ; and that the death which He suffered in atoning for sin, was not extinction, nor a cessation of thought, feeling and volition ; but "destruction from the presence of God [the Father] and from the glory of His power," the precise penalty, in kind, which awaits all the finally impenitent, and which is already the punishment of fallen angels ; and that His physical death merely marked the awful depth and completion of Atonement suffering.

Any one who will properly observe these four points will see that there is no ground whatever for the above mentioned cavil. Yet to meet this cavil, some Christians apparently not well informed on these points, have endeavored to separate between the human and the Divine in our Savior, and have attributed all His suffering to the human part alone. They have asserted that Divinity did not and could not suffer; and have quoted in their support a saying of the "fathers," "He died as He was man, but died not as He was God," an expression never intended to be thus abused. When asked, "How can we have in the great sacrifice a propitiation for the whole world, if only a human being suffered? they have answered, that although only the humanity of Christ could suffer, His sufferings derive an infinite value from the intimate union of His humanity with His Divinity, an explanation which does not explain, or which, at least, does not prove Divine impassibility.

"What God hath joined together let not man put asunder." "It is Christ that died;" and Christ was at once God and man, in mysterious and wonderful union. This is the Messiah who was the subject of type and prophecy, and promise, and apostolic testimony; and none of these, I think, warrant us in making such divisions or distinctions as would preclude the belief that the Godhead suffered.

There may be in us an aversion to thinking that God could suffer; yet, as set forth in the

Scriptures, it is not unreasonable. If in other respects the Almighty subjects Himself to limitations, why not in this? We say God is omnipresent; yet there is certainly a moral realm from which He withholds His presence, or from which He is excluded. Otherwise He could not say, " Behold I stand at the door and knock." We say that He is omnipotent; yet He has placed a limitation upon the exercise of His own power, by creating moral beings who may resist His will. We say that He is absolutely free; yet He has put Himself under obligation by His promises. He has freely offered to be bound by a covenant. Every man acknowledges this when he performs the conditions of a Divine promise and expects its fulfillment.

Why then may not such a One place Himself under such conditions as would make it possible for Him to suffer? Is such a thought more difficult than that of the incarnation, which, though we cannot understand it, we yet believe in as a fact?

But what saith the Scripture?

1—Observe that pleasure, grief and other emotions are, thoughout the Scriptures, attributed to the Divine Being;* and that He is constantly pre-

---

*(a) Love. Jno. 3. 16; 17. 24. (b) Hate. Is. 61. 8; Zech. 8. 17. (c) Joy. Neh. 8. 10; Ps. 149. 4; Is. 53. 10. (d) Pain. Ps. 78. 40; Eph. 4. 30.

sented to us as a personality exercising thought, feeling and volition.   Divest Him of this personality, and love to God becomes quite impossible.

2—Note the unequivocal language in which the Epistle to the Hebrews declares the Deity of Christ: "But unto the Son He saith, Thy throne, O God, is forever and ever."*   "And, Thou, Lord, in the beginning has laid the foundation of the earth, and the heavens are the works of thy hands."† Observe that this harmonizes exactly with Jesus' own declarations respecting Himself.   "If David then call Him Lord, how is He his son?‡   "I and my Father are one."§ Observe also that this is the same being of whom the apostle states, that He "was made a little lower than the angels *for the suffering of death*, that He by the grace of God should taste death for every man."**   And again, "It became Him for whom are all things, and by whom are all things, in bringing many sons unto glory, to make the Captain of their salvation perfect through *sufferings*."††   And further, "Inasmuch then as the children are partakers of flesh and blood, He also Himself likewise took part of the same, that through death He might destroy him that had the power of death."‡‡

---

*Heb. 1. 8. †Heb. 1. 10. ‡Mat. 22. 45. §Jno. 10. 30. **Heb. 2. 9. ††Heb. 2. 10. ‡‡Heb. 2. 14.

Who is the Captain of our salvation, a human being or God? And who *suffered* for us, a finite being or an Infinite? And who purposely *partook* of flesh and blood, "that through death He might destroy him that had the power of death?" Was it humanity or Divinity? It seems impossible that any impartial person should read the Epistle to the Hebrews, and doubt for a moment that it declares in the most clear and positive manner, that the Atonement suffering which purchased salvation for us, was endured by God the Son in His own Divine person and character.

This view is supported by much other Scripture, and antagonizes none. It abounds in assurance to the seeking soul. It calls forth the endless and ever deepening gratitude of the redeemed. It throws a flood of light upon Scripture teaching. It satisfies perfectly the demands of fallen humanity. Finally, it more highly exalts God in our love and esteem than any other conception of the Atonement; because:

1—It exhibits more clearly and perfectly the absolute, unchanging justice of God.

2—It indicates more perfectly His holiness, and His abhorrence of sin.

3—It exalts beyond all comparison His wisdom, power and love.

4—It presents the Savior in all His infinite majesty as the sympathizing friend whom we need in temptation.

5—It exhibits as nothing else can do, the boundless sufficiency of the Atonement for salvation.

APPENDIX J.

THE UNPARDONABLE SIN.

ONE specific sin alone is mentioned in the New Testament as being in its very nature beyond the power of pardon, viz.: the blasphemy against the Holy Spirit. Mat. 12. 31, 32; Mk. 3. 28, 29; Lu. 12. 10. The words of Christ, "neither in this world, nor in that which is to come," are an emphatic *never*. Even if we substitute the word *age* for the word " world," and if we regard the expression as proverbial in the time of our Savior, we are in simple justice bound to admit that the words mean *never*. Mark evidently understood it so, for he plainly says, " hath *never* forgiveness.'

It is important to know what this sin is, partly because sincere inquirers, and even devout believers, are sometimes tempted to think they have committed this sin, when they have not. This sin "was a direct insult, abuse, or evil speaking against the Holy Ghost." "It was a wanton and blasphemous attack on the Divine power and nature of Christ," or rather "against the Spirit by which He wrought His miracles." [Barnes on Mat. 12, 31, 32.] It is a great mistake to regard every sin against the Holy Spirit as blasphemy against the Holy Spirit. For anyone who is truly desirous of knowing and doing the will of God, to imagine that he has committed this sin, is therefore only a delusion of the Enemy, and should not be indulged for a moment by such a one. Yet those who are truly awakened and desirous of salvation, are more likely to entertain the thought than any other class of persons. The reason is plain. When a soul is truly in earnest about its salvation, and the answer to prayer seems to be delayed, or some other form of trial comes, Satan is ready and eager to suggest that this individual soul has committed the unpardonable sin. Let no seeking soul be taken in such a snare, and suffer needlessly. Still it is well for those who willingly indulge in sin, to be reminded that, "From its very nature, every sin tends toward blasphemy, and every blasphemy toward blasphemy against the Holy Spirit." Doubtless many will be finally condemned who have not

formally committed this sin. "Except ye be converted and become as little children, ye shall not
enter into the kingdom of heaven." "Repent and
be converted, that your sins may be blotted out."

APPENDIX K.

ERRORS ABOUT THE BLOOD.

IN the Museum of Fine Arts in Boston, among
many other Roman Catholic devices, is a paint-
ing which represents Jesus upon the cross; a large
stream of blood, like the stream of water from a
pump, spouting from His side into a stone trough;
and a pious monk stooping to the trough to fill his
pitcher.

Such gross and flagrant misrepresentations of
Scripture truth are revolting to all well-instructed
Christians. Yet many Protestants—not many ministers, perhaps—use expressions almost as misleading
as this foolish picture. "O for one drop of the
Savior's blood!" "O now I see the crimson tide."
"The cleansing stream I see, I see; I plunge and
lo! it cleanses me!" "Now I feel the blood applied." These and numerous like expressions are
liable to obscure rather than to impress the great
central truth of Christianity. Some of these expressions are perhaps based upon figures used in the

Bible, and are harmless—nay, even helpful—to such as know their figurative meaning. The mistake lies in using them when plain, unfigured statement is needed, or where the literal facts upon which the figures are based are not well understood. Such expressions thus serve to develop the unscriptural idea of a mechanical application of material blood for the cleansing of a soul.

In opposing this ignorant and mistaken conception, some zealous persons—themselves ignorant of the true meaning of redemption—have put upon the doctrine a foolish, forceless, mystical interpretation. A minister was heard to say, "Does any one suppose that we are saved by those drops of blood which fell down from our Savior's side into the ground and perished? We are saved by the *spiritual* blood." Alas, what nonsense! One of his hearers, however, reminded him that "spiritual blood" is a contradiction in terms, since a spirit has no blood. Some of his hearers afterward fell into a controversy over the statement that some of the Savior's blood "fell into the ground and perished." Some considered the statement heterodox, as denying the Divinity of Christ. It was an unnecessary and unwarrantable statement, of course; but whichever way it was settled, could have nothing to do with proving or disproving the Divinity of our Lord. That sublime doctrine rests upon a firmer foundation than any human reasoning, the word of God which endureth forever, and is abundantly corroborated by the cloud of witnesses who have put that word to the experimental test through repentance toward God and faith in our Lord Jesus Christ. Some thought that if a drop of the Savior's blood could perish, certainly His blood could not have saving efficacy. This thought also shows a very imperfect apprehension of the nature of salvation or of the atonement. To one who understands the doctrine, such discussions seem trivial, if not irreverent. The hope of salvation rests not upon any material substance, however exalted its nature or its association, nor upon any spiritual substance either, but upon the accomplished fact that the Son of God has suffered for us "the chastisement of our peace," the "stripes" due to "our transgressions," "that we by his poverty might be made rich;" that we "might receive the forgiveness of sins, and inheritance among them that are sanctified," by repentance toward God and faith in our Lord Jesus Christ; that the Just has suffered for the unjust, and the Infinite One for the finite; that having thus borne in His own person the penalty of our transgressions, He is able to intercede for us with the Father; that He ever liveth to make intercession for us; and that in view of His perfect offering, God may and does *offer* salvation to all who will repent and believe. We repeat, further, that the great atonement reached its completeness in "the offering of the *body* of Jesus Christ" by the *shedding of His blood;* and that therefore the expressions "saved by the blood," "washed in the blood," redeemed "by the precious blood," "sanctified by the offering of the body of Jesus Christ," etc., are but the plain, simple, full confession that our salvation is purchased for us by *the sacrificial death* of the Son of God.

Some have made a very sad mistake by using in an improper way the Old Testament expression, "The blood is the life." Deut. 12. 23. They have used these words as indicating that salvation comes through the life of Christ without His death; in other words, that any one who conscientiously seeks to follow the example and teachings of Christ will find salvation in this attempted imitation; or, as others think, since Christ "lighteth every man," Christ lives in every man, and this life within saves, or may save, every man. For such ideas the

Bible furnishes no foundation, and those who hold
such notions are mistaken. When the Law says
(Lev. 17, 11) "It is the blood that maketh atonement for the soul," no intelligent reader would
affirm that reference is had to the blood as it
courses through the system and ministers to the
vital functions; but to the blood *shed, poured out,
the sign of death.* When the apostle says (Rom.
5. 10), "Being reconciled, we shall be saved by His
life," his point is, that as His death has reconciled
us to God, making our salvation possible, His life,
as our High Priest and Intercessor, our Prince
and Captain, *assures* salvation to all who come
unto God by Him.

But of all the errors upon this subject there is
none more sad than the *forgetfulness* into which
regenerate persons allow themselves to fall. They
plead for God's blessings and enjoy them when received, but become so occupied with these, and
with their so-called Christian work, that they fail
to recall daily and vividly the *cost of their redemption.* No wonder that such Christians grow cold,
lifeless, proud, over-sensitive, fruitless. They do
not dwell " in the secret place of the Most High."
Those memorable words in Exodus 12. 13, " When
I see the blood, I will pass over you, " have a pres-

ent significance to the saint as well as to the sinner. Calamities come to believers, and come as judgments too, because they have ceased to dwell at the mercy-seat, *under the blood*, taking their cross *daily* and following Christ. There is no state in grace so exalted as to render it unnecessary or unhelpful to remember daily the cost of our redemption. No thought so humbles us, none so exalts the love of God for us, none so warns or so inspires; and when this thought lives and works in us, as the Holy Spirit would have it do, Christ is our effectual refuge. Calamities come not, for "all things work together for good" to us. "There shall no evil befall thee." We are always then on praying ground, for we ask nothing in our own name. We are on believing ground, for we reckon that we are nothing, and that Christ is all; we are always surrendered to death for Jesus' sake, and always trusting Him for the great salvation and its blessed fruits. "As ye have received Christ Jesus the Lord, so walk ye in Him."

APPENDIX L.

CHRIST AND THE CHILDREN.

IN the entire scope of Christian theology, there are few themes of deeper interest than the relation in which children stand to God, through the Atonement wrought by Jesus Christ. There are few themes a right understanding of which could add more vigor and efficiency to the efforts of parents, teachers and ministers to save souls. Observe the following points carefully, and see whether they do not furnish fresh and powerful incentives to soul-winning:

1—"Death came by sin"—"death" in the sense of separation from God—and this meant the loss of power to enjoy communion with God, to discern spiritual things, to live a life of holiness or even to admire it. It meant the loss of the Divine image and of sonship, as these are presented in the Scriptures. But it had a positive as well as a negative meaning. It meant a union with Satan, the prince of darkness, a service of sin, an unconscious antagonism to the will and moral attributes of God, becoming conscious when that will and those attributes were made known.

Read Rom. 3. 9-19, for a faithful description of man considered apart from the work of redemption.

Read Gal. 5. 19-21, for the *fruits* of the natural man.

2—The state of darkness, blindness, death, sinfulness, into which Adam fell, must, by natural law alone, have been the state of his posterity.

3—That it *is not* the state of infants, is clearly shown by the teachings of the Scriptures. While it is made certain that by natural law, or "by nature," "all were dead " ("in Adam all die"), it is made equally certain that little children are in a state of spiritual life. Read thoughtfully the following references:

Eph. 2. 1 (R. V.), "When ye were dead through your trespasses and sins;" and 2. 5, "When we were dead through our trespasses." Certainly if we are dead through our trespasses, we must have been alive before our trespasses. In our infancy we were not under law, for we could not apprehend law; and "when there is no law, sin is not imputed."

Rom. 7. 9, "For I was alive without the Law once; but when the commandment came, sin revived, and I died." Paul could not have given a clearer statement than this, to show that infants are alive to God, and that those who reach the years of accountability sin, and become dead through their own transgression. Yet Paul is ever clear that life, in the evangelical sense, does not come by nature, but by grace.

John 1. 9, "That was the true light which lighteth every man coming into the world," or (margin) "as he cometh into the world." But "the natural man receiveth not the things of the Spirit of God * * neither can he know them, because they are spiritually discerned." Christ, therefore, "lighteth every man coming into the world" by imparting to him spiritual life. "The LIFE was the light of men." Hence the quick discernment of innocent children, in spiritual things; more quick, by far, than when these same children have forfeited the blessed life by deliberate sin.

Mark 9. 37, "Whosoever shall receive one of such little children in my name, receiveth me." Compare this with Jesus' statement to the apostles, "He that receiveth you, receiveth me." Nowhere does Jesus use such expressions respecting the unsaved. Little children are classed with the justified, and may be received in Jesus' name; and those who thus receive them, receive Him.

Mat. 18. 3, "Except ye turn and become as little children, ye shall in no wise enter into the kingdom of heaven." It stultifies the meaning of Jesus to say that He means merely to become gentle, teach-

able, obedient, humble, etc., these qualities being
by no means uniformly exhibited by little children.
The deeper meaning is doubtless here intended
which harmonizes with other teachings of Scripture
on the same subject.

Mat. 18. 10, " See that ye despise not one of
these little ones ; for I say unto you, that in heaven
their angels do always behold the face of my Father
which is in heaven."

Compare this with Heb. 1. 14.   " Are they (the
angels) not all ministering spirits, sent forth to do
service for the sake of them that shall inherit salvation ?"   The comparison at least strongly suggests
that the little children are " heirs of salvation."

4—But this wonderful truth must not be so held
as to exclude or limit that other truth, applicable to
all *accountable* persons.   " If we say we have not
sinned, we make Him a liar." On reaching the age
of accountability, all men sin and come short of the
glory of God. The Holy Ghost, through the Scriptures, is the infallible witness to this fact ; and the
growing up of the child in favor with God, without
being " born again," is a thought which has no
foundation in the Scriptures, except in the case of
Jesus, who is as plainly declared to have been

without sin, as all other accountable human beings are declared to have sinned.

5—The age at which a child becomes accountable, or, in other words, capable of a deliberate transgression against God, depends very much upon the amount and kind of its religious instruction. Evidently some reach this age and become conscious of sin very early—at three or four years of age, perhaps younger.

6—The minister needs have no hesitation in affirming the salvation of those who die in infancy.

7—The plain, simple spiritual truths of Christianity should be clearly taught to infant classes. They will apprehend and apply them far better, and remember them far more helpfully, than if they hear them only after they have become transgressors. Every experienced teacher knows how much more receptive is a saved soul than an unsaved. Let the little child be taught that God loves him; that that which tenders his heart as he thinks of God and of duty, is the Holy Spirit Himself; that God is always displeased with sin, and that those who sin cannot enjoy the same happy communion with God as those who always obey Him; that all our good, kind, loving thoughts come from God to us; while evil thoughts and feelings are from the wicked one; that when we have sinned and separated ourselves from God, we can only return by repentance toward God and faith in Jesus Christ; that *unless* we do so return, we shall be *forever* separated; and then the exceeding blessedness of returning, as contrasted with the sorrows of endless sin.

These and kindred truths little children learn easily, and early show "the work of the law written in their hearts," and a sweet work of grace in addition to this.

8—It is an inestimable advantage to the child to reach the age of accountability while yet in his tender years, before actions and states which are contrary to the Divine will have acquired the power of habits. Conversion will thus be likely to occur in those tender years, and the child may be truly brought up "in the nurture and admonition of the Lord."

9—This truth respecting the relation of little children to God, throws light upon certain questions respecting the heathen.

Even heathen children have formed in them, through the Spirit, ideals of sin and righteousness, of obligations to God and man, of peace and condemnation. When they reach accountability and sin, thus losing the life they had, those ideals will live in memory, and exert more or less influence upon moral character. And those ideals live and work by natural law; hence the apostle could say, "the Gentiles * * do *by nature* the things contained in the law," even though he knew perfectly, and taught clearly, that that which they thus did by nature, came to them by grace.

The ideals thus furnished must differ widely in clearness and accuracy, according to the instruction received by the child, and hence in the degree of their influence upon his character. But they exist in every one, and form the basis of the universal Divine appeal, not only in childhood but in later life. This enlightening work of grace in every heart, clearly accounts for the good morals and the lofty moral teachings of many heathens who were still unsaved, and were therefore not safe guides in matters of religion. But it must also fill us with compassionate longing to bring to every child, in Christian or in heathen lands, the clear light of Divine revelation. It must make us long that, as teachers of the young, we may skillfully co-operate with the work of grace in their hearts, that they may early rejoice in salvation and shine as lights in the world. If children are properly instructed in the things of God, they will, it is true, earlier sin and lose the imparted life; but they will be nearly certain to return, repent and live; and with proper care they will be *converted very early*, *wholly sanctified* very early, become *workers for Christ* early, and realize in the most perfect manner possible the precious will of God concerning them.

ANALYTICAL INDEX.

ALPHABETICAL INDEX.